DIGITAL PRESERVATION ESSENTIALS

TRENDS IN ARCHIVES PRACTICE

ARCHIVAL ARRANGEMENT AND DESCRIPTION
Module 1: *Standards for Archival Description*
Module 2: *Processing Digital Records and Manuscripts*
Module 3: *Designing Descriptive and Access Systems*

RIGHTS IN THE DIGITAL ERA
Module 4: *Understanding Copyright Law*
Module 5: *Balancing Privacy and Restrictions: Personal and Family Papers*
Module 6: *Balancing Privacy and Restrictions: Organizational, Business, and Government Records*
Module 7: *Managing Rights and Permissions*

BECOMING A TRUSTED DIGITAL REPOSITORY (Module 8)

TEACHING WITH PRIMARY SOURCES
Module 9: *Contextualizing Archival Literacy*
Module 10: *Teaching with Archives: A Guide for Archivists, Librarians, and Educators*
Module 11: *Connecting Students and Primary Sources: Cases and Examples*

DIGITAL PRESERVATION ESSENTIALS
Module 12: *Preserving Digital Objects*
Module 13: *Digital Preservation Storage*

APPRAISAL AND ACQUISITION STRATEGIES
Module 14: *Appraising Digital Records*
Module 15: *Collecting Digital Manuscripts and Archives*
Module 16: *Accessioning Digital Archives*

. . . more modules to come!

TRENDS IN
ARCHIVES
PRACTICE

DIGITAL PRESERVATION ESSENTIALS

Edited by CHRISTOPHER J. PROM
with an Introduction by KYLE R. RIMKUS

SOCIETY OF
American Archivists
CHICAGO

Society of American Archivists
www.archivists.org

© 2016 by the Society of American Archivists.

All rights reserved. No part of this publication may be reproduced, stored in a retrieval system, or transmitted in any form or by any means without prior permission from the publisher.

Library of Congress Cataloging in Publication data is on file with the publisher.

ISBN-10: 1-931666-95-4 (print)
ISBN-10: 1-931666-96-2 (eBook)
ISBN-10: 1-931666-97-0 (pdf)

Preface to
Trends in Archives Practice

Trends in Archives Practice is an exciting publishing initiative of the Society of American Archivists (SAA), but one that is firmly tied to our publishing history and to the other publications that SAA offers. For more than forty years, SAA has published manuals, guides, and other resources that provide core knowledge concerning archival theories, practices, and procedures. Students, archivists, and people in related information professions have used publications like those in our Archival Fundamentals Series to hone their skills and to build forward-looking archival programs.

Trends in Archives Practice both complements and extends the core archival knowledge and practice that SAA has provided for these past decades. At its heart, it is an open-ended series of modules featuring brief, authoritative treatments that are written and edited by top-level professionals. Each module treats a discrete topic relating to the practical management of archives and manuscript collections in the digital age, and modules are available in both print and electronic formats.

The goal of this approach is to build agile, user-centered resources that fill significant gaps in the archival literature and that are too specialized for deep treatment in other volumes, such as those in our Archival Fundamentals Series. Many modules are planned, and readers are invited to mix, match, and combine modules that best satisfy their needs and interests. Modules in this series should be regarded as essential reading for students and practicing archivists alike, as well as for anyone who wants to begin applying archival practices to information management problems.

Trends in Archives Practice builds upon SAA's publishing traditions during a time when archival work has grown increasingly complex and fluid. In the light of rapid changes to communication and documentation patterns, students, archivists, and other information professionals need to continually refresh their knowledge and skills.

Yet a simple problem confronts anyone wanting to build competence in the areas covered by this series: an ever-growing and sometimes intractable literature. Technical standards, research reports, and case studies multiply with each technological advance. New concepts, approaches, technologies, and services emerge at a rapid pace. The ground shifts rapidly. It is easy to become unbalanced amid the complex writings and confusing acronyms, and it is SAA's firm conviction that students and practicing archivists need access to the kind of filtered and synthesized information provided by Trends in Archives Practice.

Each module will offer a convenient point of departure into a difficult area of practice, providing a general introduction to a specific field based on the following guiding principles:

- The information provided will represent the best of current practice and will make only limited reference to debates about the more theoretical aspects of archival work.
- Each module will (1) review issues related to a discrete topic; (2) discuss relevant standards, policies, practices, procedures, tools, technologies, and services; (3) describe current activities; (4) provide practical recommendations; and (5) point to other resources of value, both within the new series and in the broader literature.
- The advice provided will be appropriate for implementation in a wide range of repositories (in terms of size, focus, and available resources).
- Modules will stand on their own but may be grouped with other modules to constitute a book-length cluster.
- The content of all modules and clusters will be thoroughly peer reviewed and edited and will make an enduring contribution to the profession.

Taken as a whole, SAA's Publications Program seeks to help students, practicing archivists, and other people to develop the perspectives, knowledge, and skills that advance archival goals, both personal and corporate. We are proud that you have become part of that story by purchasing a module or cluster in Trends in Archives Practice, and we look forward to serving as your first stop for professional development, now and in the future!

CHRISTOPHER J. PROM
SAA Publications Editor

Nota Bene

This text contains a glossary of technical vocabulary or common words that are used with a specialized meaning. Within each module, the first use of terms listed in the glossary is printed in **bold** type.

Table *of* Contents

INTRODUCTION
DIGITAL PRESERVATION:
A CHALLENGE FOR OUR TIME • 1
KYLE R. RIMKUS

MODULE 12
PRESERVING DIGITAL OBJECTS • 5
ERIN O'MEARA AND KATE STRATTON

MODULE 13
DIGITAL PRESERVATION STORAGE • 75
ERIN O'MEARA AND KATE STRATTON

INTRODUCTION

Digital Preservation: A Challenge for Our Time

KYLE R. RIMKUS

Archives and libraries stand at a turning point. Publishers and distributors of books, periodicals, music, and motion pictures are moving away from the manufacture and sale of discrete, tangible items in favor of licensing network access to electronic texts, articles, songs, and videos. Although we have not seen a wholesale shift to digital distribution for all media types—physical books, for example, still hold a strong market position relative to e-books—the transition from analog to digital has nevertheless been decisive.

This shift is especially true for materials typically collected by archives and manuscript libraries. Personal and corporate records in the form of correspondence, photographs, and financial documents no longer necessarily exist as items one may hold in hand and file away. They live on computer drives and web servers, frequently in cloud services where they do not even belong, strictly speaking, to the people who created them.

Our personal hard drives of photos, videos, music, and email; government agencies' electronic records of communication and decision-making; publishers' collections of electronic books and periodicals; universities' servers of research data—all of these must overcome a host of risks if they are to be of use to future generations. How will we retain a record of life, culture, governance, and knowledge in the networked digital era?

The field of digital preservation confronts the many challenges implied by this question, and much depends on that field's success in developing models and practices to meet them, as well as on how archives and manuscript libraries implement those practices. As a preservation librarian, it strikes me that this challenge has provoked its share of anxiety in the archives field, with its established traditions for managing paper documents and records. Nor has this anxiety been assuaged by practitioners of digital preservation, who heavily pepper conversation with references to SIPs, AIPs, and DIPs, OAIS reference models and TDRs. Their overindulgence in acronyms and techno-jargon has made digital preservation an intimidating field—even to the so-called experts.

While we may hope this situation will change, it is unfortunately impossible to understand digital preservation in its present form without acquiring some fluency in abstruse concepts and their associated lingo. The two modules in this volume, both capably authored by Erin O'Meara and Kate Stratton, do not blindly repeat or abuse the specialized terminology which is so rampant in digital preservation literature. Rather, they define the necessary terms succinctly and articulate key concepts in a clear, comprehensible way.

Module 12: Preserving Digital Objects presents a bird's eye view of the field, fit to serve as both a gentle introduction as well as a reference text for seasoned professionals. It includes a brief review of key literature in the field, beginning with concerns expressed in the 1980s and 1990s about the long-term durability of digital content. As archivists realized they could not simply retrofit established practices for the arrangement, description, and preservation of print and other analog formats, they collaborated with those in other fields—such as information and computer science—to develop a new digital paradigm. The tools and standards that emerged from this period include the National Digital Stewardship Alliance's Levels of Preservation, the Open Archival Information System Reference Model, and the concept of a Trustworthy Digital Repository. In describing all of these, O'Meara and Stratton use clear language to communicate difficult concepts in a straightforward manner, discussing working practices that every archivist and digital preservationist must master. Their overview extends to the transfer of content from obsolete media carriers, the tools of digital forensics, and file format identification and normalization.

Module 13: Digital Preservation Storage focuses on the first line of defense in any good digital preservation program—digital storage. In the preservation of books and manuscripts, a great deal depends on favorable environmental factors. Preservation officers in archives and libraries guard against extreme fluctuations in temperature, relative humidity, and the presence of pests in order to safeguard their holdings from accelerated deterioration. Likewise, digital preservationists outfit proper digital storage as the bedrock of the digital preservation services they offer.

But what is the difference between file replication and back-up? What are the relative advantages of spinning disk, tape, and solid state storage? What does it mean to monitor fixity? What storage strategy is best suited to a small, medium, or large institution? And does it make most sense to manage storage locally, in partnership with another organization, or with a contracted cloud service? *Module 13* provides excellent guidance to professionals seeking to answer such questions. The authors provide an overview of the many factors that must be addressed: documenting technical needs, determining staffing requirements, estimating costs, and ensuring sustainability. They close the module with interviews with staff from the University of California at San Diego and Chronopolis, the University of Minnesota, and Northern Illinois University, all of whom graciously share insight gained from first-hand experience in providing digital preservation services at their respective institutions.

Digital preservation is not easy. The ground is constantly shifting as we strive to ensure that the cultural record, the preponderance of which is now created, stored, and distributed digitally, does not slip through our hands and into the dustbin of history. While many people will have a knee-jerk reaction to new media formats—some condemning all things binary as ephemeral, while others presume that anything to appear online is "permanent"—such attitudes amount to little more than speculation, and are of little use to the working archivist who must maintain collections of digital materials. Rather, as archives acquire more and more collections of recent origin, a competency in digital preservation has ceased being a luxury and become instead an essential requirement. The successful archivist needs a grounding in the fundamental concepts of digital preservation, a command of its key terminology and practices, and an ability to build effective programs and practices. These modules provide an excellent point of entry.

Kyle R. Rimkus is assistant professor and preservation librarian at the University of Illinois at Urbana-Champaign Library, where he is responsible for articulating and implementing a preservation strategy for digital collections. His research focuses on assessing the long-term viability of digital formats in a broad, historical context.

MODULE 12
PRESERVING DIGITAL OBJECTS

Erin O'Meara and Kate Stratton

Module 12 Contents

Introduction • 8
    A Digital Preservation Program: Starting Small and Building Out • 12
    Improve Storage Architecture • 15
    Map Preservation Activities by Content Type/Format • 15

Preservation of Digital Objects: Applying Standards • 16
    Open Archival Information System (OAIS) Reference Model • 16
        The Submission Information Package: Preparing to Preserve • 19
        The Archival Information Package: What is an AIP? • 23
    ISO 16363: A Related Standard for Trusted Digital Repositories • 28

Preservation Actions in Context • 30
    Digital Object Description and Management • 32
    Other Tools • 36

Summary and Recommendations • 37

Appendices
    Appendix A: Further Readings • 39
    Appendix B: Case Studies • 44
        Case Study 1: Rockefeller Archive Center • 44
        by Sibyl Schaefer
        Case Study 2: University of North Carolina–Chapel Hill • 51
        by Jill Sexton, Meg Tuomala, and Gregory Jansen
    Appendix C: Preservation Metadata and Its Tools • 58
    Appendix D: Metadata Schema Examples • 61
    Appendix E: Glossary • 71

ABOUT THE AUTHORS

Erin O'Meara is head of the Office of Digital Innovation and Stewardship at the University of Arizona Libraries. Her research interests include ethnographic approaches to data management and recordkeeping, digital preservation, and archives leadership. She has previously worked at Gates Archive, the University of North Carolina at Chapel Hill, and the University of Oregon. O'Meara received her master of archival studies from the University of British Columbia in 2004. While at UBC, she conducted research for the InterPARES 2 Project pertaining to archaeological records managed in Geographic Information Systems.

Kate Stratton is the collection development archivist at Gates Archive in Seattle, Washington, where she oversees donor relations and acquisitions. Prior to joining Gates Archive in 2013, Stratton worked at the Stuart A. Rose Manuscript, Archives, and Rare Book Library at Emory University. She earned a master of science in library science from the School of Library and Information Science at the University of North Carolina at Chapel Hill in 2010.

Introduction

Archival repositories increasingly include digital objects such as word processing documents, graphics, images, email messages, web pages, databases and datasets among their holdings, in both born-digital and digitized formats. Unlike paper-based archival materials, these digital objects cannot be accessed or understood by humans without the use of a machine.

Digital objects are simply pieces of binary code, sequenced strings of 1s and 0s, otherwise known as bitstreams. Written to a medium such as disk or tape, they are read by machines and interpreted by other pieces of binary code—what we call software. Rendering a digital object and making it interpretable by a human (for example, as a set of many colored pixels that together make a recognizable image on a screen) requires all of these components and interactions. Damage or loss to any component could make the object practically, if not permanently, inaccessible. To mitigate the risk of loss, it is imperative that archivists take proactive and systematic action to preserve digital objects and the many components that are necessary to render them and to make them interpretable.

Preservation is the set of activities, processes, and policies that safeguard materials, preventing, where possible, deterioration, damage, or loss in order to enable ongoing access to the information, artifacts, and evidence that comprise archival collections. To preserve digital objects, the activities, processes, and policies involved must account for the unique characteristics of digital content as described above.

Archivists are required to preserve the digital objects in their collections and confront the need for new knowledge, skills, technologies, strategies, and practices. These challenges, coupled with those inherent in digital objects, can seem daunting. The maturation of digital preservation as a discipline, pioneering archival research, and practical testing of tools make preservation an attainable goal for organizations of various sizes and levels of resources.

This module synthesizes what theorists and practitioners have to say about how to preserve digital objects and will explore concepts, standards, and systems, rooting them in practical examples. It will focus on digital object management processes and outline the elements of the Archival Information Package (AIP), an intentional, machine-understandable grouping of files that includes both digital archival content and all of the information (i.e., metadata) necessary to understand, use, and authenticate the content. The module will review AIP components, translate them into archival terms, and illustrate the key elements with examples. The module will also address the tools and systems available to facilitate long-term management of the AIP, keeping the package and its data files safe and useable over time. Finally, the module will provide case studies of digital preservation system implementations at two archival institutions, demonstrating the convergence of authentic digital objects, preservation metadata, tools, and systems to enable successful long-term preservation. Because the module is centrally concerned with the preservation and management of digital objects it assumes, as a precursor, that the objects in question have been acquired according to archival best practices.[1] This module will prepare archivists to create workflows and processes, analyze tools, and implement systems in order to preserve and make accessible digital objects held in their repositories.

Techniques for long-term preservation of traditional paper-based archival objects are well established and broadly adopted. Mary Lynn Ritzenthaler's *Preserving Archives and Manuscripts* comprehensively codifies archival thinking in this area.[2] While no canonically analogous work yet exists in the digital preservation space, archival theorists and practitioners have been defining the components and building the foundation for more than two decades.

It is difficult to pinpoint the archivist's first encounter with digital records as collection material, but it is in the 1980s and 1990s, responding to the 1970s arrival of the personal computer, that there is an uptick in discussion of digital records in the archival literature. In the 1980s and 1990s, the archival community noted the expansion of digital content creation and began to acknowledge the challenges ahead. Edward Weldon, in his 1982 presidential address to the Society

---

1 For readings on the sound acquisition of digital archival objects, see the "Demystifying Born Digital" OCLC reports including Julianna Barrera-Gomez and Ricky Erway, *Walk This Way: Detailed Steps for Transferring Born-Digital Content from Media You Can Read In-house* (Dublin, OH: OCLC Research, 2013), http://www.oclc.org/content/dam/research/publications/library/2013/2013-02.pdf, captured at https://perma.cc/GBN6-WLXL; and J. Gordon Daines, "Processing Digital Records and Manuscripts," in *Archival Arrangement and Description*, ed. Christopher J. Prom and Thomas J. Frusciano (Chicago: Society of American Archivists, 2012), 90–143.

2 Chicago: Society of American Archivists, 2010.

of American Archivists, discussed the "post-industrial, electronic information revolution," and gave voice to a growing uncertainty: "What the ultimate impact of the computer will be upon archives and archivists is unknown."[3] Archival theorists responded to this uncertainty with predictions. Some predicted that unconstrained practices of records creators in the digital realm would translate to complexities in understanding, authenticating, and managing digital records once they reached the archives. John McDonald noted that the digital recordkeeping environment is like "the wild frontier" with "no rules of the road."[4] Luciana Duranti observed that this no-rules approach "produced the sloppiest records creation ever in the history of record making" and expressed concern over the authenticity and reliability of records created in such context.[5] Contemporaneously, Jeff Rothenberg, noticing the rapid pace of technological change, brought attention to the concept of format obsolescence.[6] Subsequent authors expanded the understanding of threats to digital objects to include physical deterioration, damage, bit rot, and hardware obsolescence. These concerns gave rise to interest in digital preservation.

In the intervening decades, pioneering preservationists continued to develop, debate, and refine theory and practice. In 1998, Margaret Hedstrom documented then-current digital preservation techniques, such as printing to paper or microfilm, identifying their inadequacies in preserving dynamic data objects from complex systems.[7] Despite this work, digital preservation remains largely under-implemented at a systemic level. Rachel Onuf and Tom Hyry noted in 2011 that with few exceptions, archivists have failed to adjust to the new digital reality

---

3   Edward Weldon, "Archives and the Challenges of Change," *The American Archivist* 46, no. 2 (Spring 1983): 125–134, doi: http://dx.doi.org/10.17723/aarc.46.2.g91733970404m01p.
4   John McDonald, "Managing Records in the Modern Office: Taming the Wild Frontier," *Archivaria* 39 (1995): 70, http://journals.sfu.ca/archivar/index.php/archivaria/article/download/12069/13047, captured at https://perma.cc/GJZ7-SQ4Z.
5   Luciana Duranti, "Reliability and Authenticity: The Concepts and Their Implications," *Archivaria* 39 (1995): 9, http://journals.sfu.ca/archivar/index.php/archivaria/article/viewFile/12063/13035, captured at https://perma.cc/494J-S649.
6   Jeff Rothenberg, "Ensuring the Longevity of Digital Documents," *Scientific American* 272, no. 1 (1995): 4–29, http://www.scientificamerican.com/article/ensuring-the-longevity-of-digital-d/, captured at https://perma.cc/UE2U-MFS3.
7   See Margaret Hedstrom, "Digital Preservation: A Time Bomb for Digital Libraries," *Computers and the Humanities* 31 (1998): 195–196, http://deepblue.lib.umich.edu/bitstream/handle/2027.42/42573/?sequence=1; and H. Heslop, S. Davis, and A. Wilson, *An Approach to the Preservation of Digital Records* (Canberra: National Archives of Australia, 2002).

in their acquisition and preservation of materials.[8] In his Society of American Archivists presidential address, Richard Pearce-Moses strongly encouraged archivists to be courageous with digital content and technology, and, importantly, to take action.[9]

The archival community has responded with publications emphasizing real world strategies and step-by-step instructions. At an organizational level, the AIMS project developed a high-level framework for stewardship of digital archival materials, emphasizing cross-institutional collaboration and skill development.[10] The PARADIGM project from the Universities of Oxford and Manchester explored all aspects of collecting born-digital private papers.[11]

Literature also amassed around specific file formats and more complicated types of digital content with unique preservation concerns. For example, the Digital Preservation Coalition published Technology Watch Reports, in-depth introductions for preservation practitioners, on preserving email, eBooks and eJournals, websites, and geospatial data, among other special topics.[12] The reports track changes in the field as it develops and help lower the barriers to broader participation in digital preservation. There have been several recently published analyses of preservation policies across organizations that evaluate file format policies, service levels provided within digital preservation programs, as well as overall program descriptions.[13]

---

8   Rachel Onuf and Tom Hyry, "Take It Personally: The Implications of Personal Records in Electronic Form," in *I, Digital: Personal Collections in the Digital Era*, ed. Christopher A. Lee (Chicago: Society of American Archivists, 2011).
9   Richard Pearce-Moses, "Janus in Cyberspace: Archives on the Threshold of the Digital Era," *The American Archivist* 70 (2007): 13–22, doi: http://americanarchivist.org/doi/abs/10.17723/aarc.70.1.n7121165223j6t83.
10 AIMS Work Group, *AIMS Born-Digital Collections: An Inter-Institutional Model for Stewardship*, 2012, http://dcs.library.virginia.edu/aims/white-paper/, captured at https://perma.cc/9E3J-8SCH.
11 PARADIGM, "Project Overview." Last modified February 18, 2008.http://www.paradigm.ac.uk/about/index.html, captured at http://www.webarchive.org.uk/wayback/archive/20081001093108/http://www.paradigm.ac.uk/workbook/pdfs/index.html.
12 Digital Preservation Coalition, "DPC Technology Watch Reports: ISSN 2048-7916," http://www.dpconline.org/publications/technology-watch-reports.
13 Kyle Rimkus, "Digital Preservation File Format Policies of ARL Member Libraries: An Analysis," *D-Lib Magazine* 20, no. 3/4 (2014), http://www.dlib.org/dlib/march14/rimkus/03rimkus.html, captured at https://perma.cc/4BN3-6XJG; Barbara Sierman, Catherine Jones, Sean Bechhofer, and Gry Elstrøm, "Preservation Policy Levels in SCAPE," in *iPRES 2013: Proceedings of the 10th International Conference on Preservation of Digital Objects*, eds. José Borbinha, Michael Nelson, and Steve Knight, http://purl.pt/24107/1/iPres2013_PDF/Preservation%20Policy%20Levels%20in%20SCAPE.pdf, captured at https://perma.cc/FHQ7-5XR9; and Madeline Sheldon et al., "Analysis of Current Digital Preservation Policies," http://www.digitalpreservation.gov/documents/Analysis of Current Digital Preservation Policies.pdf, captured at https://perma.cc/4Q6X-XJZA.

Archival practitioners have also shared their emerging digital preservation implementations through case studies and other analysis of practice. Michael Forstrom provided real-life analysis from the Beinecke's manuscript unit of the InterPARES Authenticity Task Force report, "Requirements for Assessing and Maintaining the Authenticity of Electronic Records," as it relates to implementing *Describing Archives: A Content Standard (DACS)*.[14] Katherine Kott and Tom Cramer reflected upon the implementation success and challenges of a scholarly preservation repository.[15]

Additional work has been done to address the sound acquisition of digital archival objects, focusing on protecting integrity and authenticity and facilitating the success of preservation efforts. The "Demystifying Born Digital" reports from OCLC Research suggested practical approaches and provided step-by-step instructions for assessing and acquiring born-digital objects from current or legacy media.[16] J. Gordon Daines similarly proposed workflows for digital content from acquisition and accession to arrangement and description.[17]

These more recent publications demonstrate growing comfort and maturity in the profession as it relates to born-digital materials. We can see the transition from initial wariness, to theoretical, and finally, practical engagement. Work remains to be done, however, in filling out the practical advice and strategies for managing and preserving born-digital objects in the archival context. The authors aim to contribute to the bridging of this gap in this module.

A Digital Preservation Program: Starting Small and Building Out

The preservation of digital objects is best approached incrementally, collaboratively, and iteratively. Practical approaches to begin to address basic levels of preservation can start small and build over time.

---

14 Michael Forstrom, "Managing Electronic Records in Manuscript Collections: A Case Study from the Beinecke Rare Book and Manuscript Library," *The American Archivist* 72 (2009): 460–477, http://americanarchivist.org/doi/pdf/10.17723/aarc.72.2.b82533tvr7713471.

15 Katherine Kott and Tom Cramer, "Designing and Implementing Second Generation Digital Preservation Services: A Scalable Model for the Stanford Digital Repository," *D-Lib Magazine* 16, no. 9/10 (2010), http://www.dlib.org/dlib/september10/cramer/09cramer.html, captured at https://perma.cc/46A6-MEFH.

16 Barrera-Gomez and Erway, *Walk This Way*; and Ricky Erway, *You've Got to Walk Before You Can Run: First Steps for Managing Born-Digital Content Received on Physical Media* (Dublin, OH: OCLC Research, 2012), http://www.oclc.org/research/publications/library/2012/2012-06.pdf, captured at https://perma.cc/UE95-HBRT.

17 J. Gordon Daines III, "Module 2: Processing Digital Records and Manuscripts," in *Archival Arrangement and Description*, eds. C. Prom and T. Frusciano (Chicago: Society of American Archivists, 2013).

Repositories should establish levels of digital preservation that will be applicable over time and across collections. The National Digital Stewardship Alliance's Levels of Preservation provides a good model.[18] Below is a high-level description of the levels they describe and the enhancements your institution can work toward as you build out your digital preservation program. These concepts will be discussed in more depth throughout the module.

Level 1 – Protect your data
- Get data onto a storage platform and have two complete copies
- Provide **fixity** checks for all incoming and collected digital objects
- Know who has access to your files on the server and protect the files from write access
- Inventory your holdings

Level 2 – Know your data
- Have three complete copies of data, including one geographically disparate copy
- Use write blockers on removable media
- Virus check risky content and document access restrictions to digital objects
- Know all the file formats in the holdings

Level 3 – Monitor your data
- Monitor your storage system for obsolescence
- Virus check all incoming content
- Log all fixity data and all actions performed on digital holdings
- Create standardized technical and administrative metadata
- Evaluate file format obsolescence risks on holdings

Level 4 – Repair your data
- Utilize more complex geo-redundancy of copies
- Replace any damaged objects with a healthy copy
- Audit the logs
- Create standardized preservation metadata
- Conduct format **migration** and emulation of data, as needed

---

18 NDSA's Levels of Preservation, http://ndsa.diglib.org/activities/levels-of-digital-preservation/, captured at https://perma.cc/VY8Y-S3GU.

An immediate goal of any digital preservation program should be to reach baseline levels of preservation (Level 1). As staff, financial, and technological resources become available, supplement the baseline with additional activities, processes, and technologies.

The endeavor to reach baseline levels of preservation and beyond should be approached collaboratively within and across institutions. The AIMS report notes, in relation to intra-institutional collaboration: "When dealing with born-digital materials, however, it is best to employ a more collaborative approach from the outset: technical expertise and experience with newly designed workflows (or those just being tested) from archival or digital staff will aid the curator in appraising materials, performing test captures, and identifying any issues related to accessioning, processing, preservation or delivery."[19] Similarly, Ricky Erway suggests that certain preservation activities, particularly those requiring rare or expensive hardware and software, be collaboratively sourced in the larger archival community through the support and development of "SWAT" (software and workstations for antiquated technology) sites.[20] These areas of specialization are starting to be piloted and tested,[21] but there is work to be done to build more formal centers of expertise and staffing to provide the service to external users.

Once basic acquisition and **ingest** processes and stable, adequate storage have been implemented, work toward strategy and infrastructure improvements. These improvements enable the transition from project to program.

First, strategize. Develop a basic digital preservation strategy and related documentation. A digital preservation strategy documents institutional commitment, articulates the levels of preservation an archives provides, and sets clear goals for growth. The goals and action items should create a three-year aspirational organizational vision. The British Library and University of Massachusetts Amherst Libraries

---

19 AIMS Born-Digital Collections: An Inter-Institutional Model for Stewardship, 4, http://dcs.library.virginia.edu/aims/white-paper/, captured at https://perma.cc/9E3J-8SCH.
20 Ricky Erway, *Swatting the Long Tail of Digital Media: A Call for Collaboration* (Dublin, OH: OCLC Research, 2012), http://www.oclc.org/research/publications/library/2012/2012-08.pdf, captured at https://perma.cc/LKW8-N9EA.
21 The XFR STN exhibition at the New Museum, http://www.newmuseum.org/exhibitions/view/xfr-stn, is starting to test out this SWAT approach. Captured at https://perma.cc/9JE4-4H3S.

both created clear digital preservation strategies that contain actionable goals over a specific period of time.[22]

Next, assess and advocate. Document the business impact digital preservation efforts will make as they relate to organizational goals and mission. Determine how to best articulate the benefit/value of preserving digital objects held by your repository. The Balanced Value Impact Model provides a framework for self-assessment. Some commercial digital preservation services also include risk calculators and business case templates.[23] This business impact can be used for both programmatic growth and budget justification.

Improve Storage Architecture

Develop basic and "blue sky" or ideal storage requirements based on the goals outlined in your preservation strategy. Meet basic needs, while striving to enact a blue sky/ideal scenario. Ideal storage scenarios will include stable, secure, replicated storage (could be a combination of on-premise, hosted, or distributed storage); and audit and monitoring capability for your storage (ability to control access permissions, how the data is being accessed, and file integrity; see *Module 13: Digital Preservation Storage*).

Map Preservation Activities by Content Type/Format

Considering significant properties, create preservation maps for specific content types or file formats.

- Establish basic normalization activities that will create copies of digital objects in more stable formats.
- Develop and document more complex migration strategies beyond the core file formats your archives acquires.
- Build basic environments for emulation of older formats. This would involve running a virtual machine with an older operating system to view files that do not have a common migration path into a modern file format.

---

22 British Library, *British Library Digital Preservation Strategy* (London: 2013), http://www.bl.uk/aboutus/stratpolprog/collectioncare/digitalpreservation/strategy/BL_DigitalPreservationStrategy_2013-16-external.pdf, captured at https://perma.cc/U89H-2APP. Digital Creation and Preservation Working Group, *UMass Amherst Libraries Digital Preservation Policy* (Amherst: 2011), http://www.library.umass.edu/assets/aboutus/attachments/University-of-Massachusetts-Amherst-Libraries-Digital-Preservation-Policy3-18-2011-templated.pdf, captured at https://perma.cc/D6SL-GMKT.
23 Simon Tanner, *Measuring the Impact of Digital Resources: The Balanced Value Impact Model* (King's College London, October 2012), http://www.kdcs.kcl.ac.uk/innovation/impact.html, captured at https://perma.cc/D6SL-GMKT.

Preservation of Digital Objects: Applying Standards

Open Archival Information System (OAIS) Reference Model

Before covering approaches to preserving digital objects in archival repositories, it is important to understand the standards and functional requirements surrounding digital preservation. Functional requirements are the necessary behaviors and processes in a system, which can help archivists evaluate and select digital preservation tools and systems. The Open Archival Information System (OAIS) Reference Model[24] and resulting ISO standard (16363)[25] are seminal documents for use in developing requirements and specifications for a digital preservation system, including individual workflows (such as ingest or access copy generation) and smaller tool implementation (like BagIt or BitCurator). They can also serve as documents to determine key characteristics needed in a system that will preserve digital objects long term. These characteristics can be used to improve an existing system or to select or develop a new one. The building blocks of OAIS can be used to articulate system features needed in your digital repository.

The OAIS Reference Model provides a common language and conceptual framework for the understanding, design, and implementation of a digital preservation system. The model represents the flow of information from ingest (process to accept content into a digital repository), to management and preservation, to retrieval and access. The model describes the various states of information as the:

- Submission Information Package (**SIP**), digital object and related information at the point of ingest;
- Archival Information Package (**AIP**), digital object and related information as it is stored and managed for preservation, and;
- Dissemination Information Package (**DIP**), the package used for retrieval and access.

The SIP, AIP, and DIP documentation can be a useful communication tool for archivists when explaining archival requirements to their information technology partners and other stakeholders or decision makers. The model can also be used to evaluate the offerings of

---

24 Consultative Committee for Space Data Systems, *Reference Model for an Open Archival Information System (OAIS)* (2012), http://public.ccsds.org/publications/archive/650x0m2.pdf, captured at https://perma.cc/4C6D-BAJA.

25 Consultative Committee for Space Data Systems, *Audit and Certification of Trustworthy Digital Repositories* (2011), http://public.ccsds.org/publications/archive/652x0m1.pdf, captured at https://perma.cc/8J63-TBEA.

Figure 1. OAIS Functional Entity Diagram

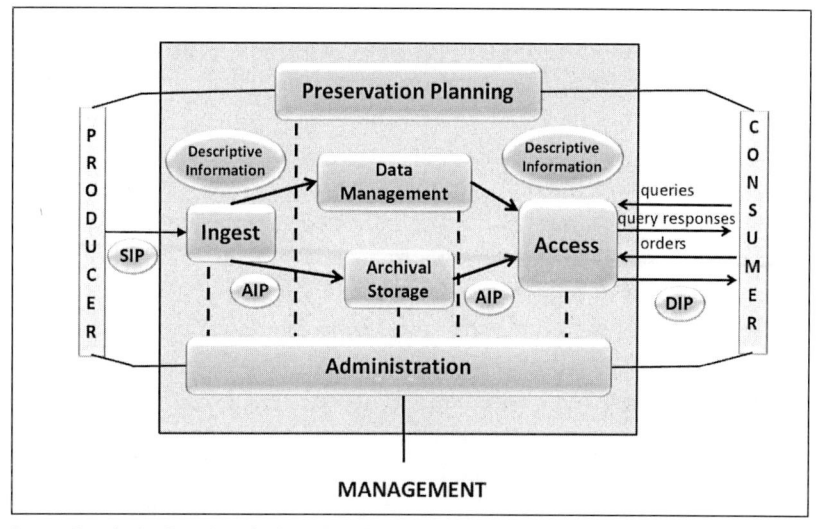

Source: Consultative Committee for Space Data Systems, 2012, page 4–1.

vendors providing digital preservation systems or services. The model accounts for and clearly presents the information flow of both the digital object and associated metadata during archival processes such as accessioning, processing, and access.

To translate OAIS terms into archival terms at a basic level, consider the following: SIP refers to packages used during acquisition. This is what an archivist receives as an accession from a donor. AIP refers to packages used during processing and storage. This is what we process and preserve over time in an archival repository, after applying descriptive and administrative metadata. DIP refers to packages used during access. This type of package is what we provide to the user, including descriptive information that places it in context amongst other materials within and across collections.

A SIP is a package of files including archival digital objects and the important information about the objects (technical, descriptive, or administrative metadata) transferred to the archives. Depending on the context of donation and local institutional practices, the SIP may be created by either the donor or the receiving archivist. With the right systems and tools in place, metadata can be requested from and provided by donors, or automatically extracted, at the time of submission. For example, archivists working with living and technically savvy donors can require that donations be submitted using packaging specifications, like BagIt. They can further define their minimal metadata requirements to be included in the bag-info.txt metadata file. An analogous, but simplified example of this approach can be seen in the process used for electronic theses and dissertations submission. Authors are required to submit files in a specified format and also to provide specific metadata (e.g., title, author name, abstract) in order to complete the submission process. At the date of publication, the Bagger Tool, developed by the Library of Congress, is the most well-established tool of this kind used by archival institutions; however, there are several ongoing research and development projects with similar aims.[26]

In the case of digital files retrieved from media carriers post-donation, the archivist will often be responsible for generating the metadata files required for a complete SIP. Forensic acquisitions software, like BitCurator, FTK Imager, Forensic Toolkit (FTK), and Guymager, are capable of extracting and reporting some technical and structural metadata from target files.[27] Most commercial digital preservation systems also include pre-ingest tools or microservices that allow archivists to extract technical metadata and provide additional descriptive or administrative metadata to be included in the submission packages. It is important that this metadata be standardized, well-structured, and machine-readable. This is achieved through adherence to defined document formats and **schemas**. Packaging metadata in **XML** is the de facto standard format, though there are varying implementation practices and schemas selected across institutions. Local schema implementation may be dictated and managed by a digital preservation system or repository software. Practitioners without an existing or planned digital preservation system or digital repository should prioritize interoperability and flexibility when selecting a format and schema in which to record their metadata. This module will discuss preservation metadata requirements and schema in greater depth in Appendix C.

---

26 Library of Congress, *Bagger*, https://github.com/LibraryOfCongress/bagger, captured at https://perma.cc/SC8N-3D8R, and *Exactly*, https://www.avpreserve.com/tools/exactly, captured at https://perma.cc/P6MN-6B6Z.

27 BitCurator is a suite of open source forensic and data analysis tools for the archival community available for download from http://www.bitcurator.net/, captured at https://perma.cc/F6QM-95BL. FTK Imager is a freeware component of the Forensic Toolkit (FTK) suite available for download from AccessData, http://www.accessdata.com/support/product-downloads, captured at https://perma.cc/7BHY-EXTX. Forensic Toolkit (FTK) is a for-purchase computer forensic software made by AccessData, http://www.accessdata.com/solutions/digital-forensics/ftk, captured at https://perma.cc/YB84-K7HM. Guymager is a free forensic imager for media acquisition available for download from http://guymager.sourceforge.net/, captured at https://perma.cc/EX63-LSST.

Preserving Digital Objects   **19**

At the point of ingest—"the process of adding objects to a preservation repository"[28]—the SIP is enhanced with additional technical, descriptive, and administrative metadata and transformed into the AIP after being placed in preservation storage. See the sidebar for an example of this process, as applied to a collection of digital photographs.

The Submission Information Package: Preparing to Preserve

As Ross Harvey noted, preservation of digital objects is informed by and reliant upon both "what comes before preservation and what comes after—that is, how the data are created and how they will be used, and by whom, in the future."[29] The creation of a preservation-ready Submission Information Package (SIP) is crucial to form long-lived digital objects. As described above, a SIP is a package of files including archival digital objects and the important information about the objects (technical, descriptive, or administrative metadata) transferred to the archives. The creation of these packages requires workflows that accurately (i.e., authentically) capture both the archival files and the relevant metadata, like **provenance** and other pre-acquisition history, that will help inform preservation activities and processing into the future. There are many data points to document or capture at the point of acquisition or data transfer that will enhance the ability to describe, migrate, and provide access to digital objects. A good set of administrative, technical, structural, and descriptive metadata elements are described as part of a well-formed AIP later in this module.

Archivists acquiring content from legacy media carriers (e.g., 3.5" floppy disks, zip drives, and optical media) interspersed within analog collections need to be able to transfer content from media in a preservation-friendly manner. At a high level, this is accomplished through documented and repeatable processes that do not alter or affect the integrity or authenticity of the content. The OCLC Demystifying Born-Digital reports provide step-by-step guidance for transferring content from digital media carriers with equipment and technical skills that are attainable for many institutions.[30]

---

28 PREMIS editorial committee, *PREMIS Data Dictionary for Preservation Metadata* version 2.2 (July 2012): 134, http://www.loc.gov/standards/premis/v2/premis-2-2.pdf, captured at https://perma.cc/2WSX-4WRC.
29 Ross Harvey, *Digital Curation: A How-To-Do-It Manual* (New York: Neal-Schuman Publishers, 2004), xvi.
30 Barrera-Gomez and Erway, *Walk This Way*.

Process of Ingest for a Collection of Digital Photographs

An archives receives a set of digital photographs from a donor, ranging in date from 1999 to 2007. The formats include high resolution TIFFs, some RAW files, and a few JPEGs. Upon basic accession of the objects, the SIP would include:
- Digital photos
- High-level description of collection contents (created by archivist or donor)
- Fixity information (i.e., **checksums** generated upon receipt of each digital object)
- Any other requirements unique to the SIP specification

The archives will ingest the SIP into archival storage either through a repository or manually; this process will include the activities necessary to create an AIP. These processes will be performed by an ingest tool or set of software applications like BagIt or Curator's Workbench, or by software embedded into larger preservation systems like Preservica, Rosetta, or Archivematica. The output should be documented and associated with the digital objects. These activities include:
- Generation of unique identifiers for all files in the new accession (e.g., universally unique identifiers or UUIDs)
- Fixity: run checksums and evaluate against original checksums after files are moved to archival storage
- Inventory: create inventory of file and folder listing (e.g., METS structmap, or path/filenames generated using a tool like Karen's Directory Printer or the NARA File Analyzer)
- **Metadata extraction**
  - File size for all files
  - File formats list for all files
  - Timestamps from files and any other embedded metadata
- Event information
  - Who ingested materials (name of archivist or staff member)
  - When materials were ingested (**timestamp**)
- File path of where digital objects came from (donor machine, original media, or transfer device) and file path where they are stored after ingest

There's an assumption here that the archives has approved this content and worked with the donor on the material that is relevant to be submitted. We do not cover issues of appraisal.

Your organization should create a SIP specification document that articulates what your SIP should contain and how it is packaged. Your SIP should be interoperable with whatever repository you are using to manage digital objects (e.g., Fedora, DSpace, etc.). Archivematica has a very simple example, https://www.archivematica.org/wiki/SIP_Structure, captured at https://perma.cc/N23Z-F82. The Harvard E-Journal Archive developed a very detailed SIP specification for a project in 2001, http://old.diglib.org/preserve/harvardsip10.pdf, captured at https://perma.cc/WHG5-HJ7P.

Some institutions with specific requirements may choose to utilize more complex capture techniques, such as those prescribed by digital forensics, when acquiring content from legacy carriers. Digital forensics is a discipline originating in law enforcement that involves the acquisition (or recovery) and analysis of digital objects for evidential purposes using file characteristics and metadata. These techniques typically capture data at a more granular level, exactly replicating bitstreams or bytes of digital objects. These techniques, such as those described in Jeremy Leighton John's "Digital Forensics and Preservation," are more technologically and resource intensive, but enable archivists to "identify privacy issues; establish a chain of custody for provenance; employ write protection for capture and transfer; and detect forgery or manipulation."[31] Archivists might use digital forensics to locate personally identifying information, such as social security and credit card numbers; prevent bytes and metadata from being changed in the original file or written to by the examining computer; and determine through analysis of metadata that a file was created at a time or by a person contrary to claims (forgery) or that bytes have been altered in an unintended or malicious way (manipulation). Digital forensics capture techniques are not required for the creation of preservation-ready packages, but it is important for archivists to be aware of their options, especially when confronting media that is unrenderable in modern systems.

Archivists working with living donors have additional opportunities to capture context about the digital objects, as well as an opportunity to develop a dialogue with the donor about best practices if there will be accruals of content over time. Through conversation with donors, archivists can understand the computing practices that created the archival objects. They also, in some instances, have the opportunity to educate donors about sustainable file formats and good file hygiene. In working with donors, archivists can also raise concerns relevant to preserving digital objects, as the PARADIGM project emphasizes, "particularly the issues of: privacy, confidentiality and data protection; access by third parties, especially by means of freedom of information requests; and IPR (Intellectual Property Rights) in the content of the

---

31 Jeremy Leighton John, "Digital Forensics and Preservation," DPC Technology Watch Report 12-03 (Digital Preservation Coalition, 2012), http://dx.doi.org/10.7207/twr12-03.

archive."[32] These activities, typically associated with digital curation, can enhance preservation metadata and ultimately the preservability and accessibility of the objects.

Examples of standards, procedures, and systems for carrying out digital acquisition activities include the Producer Archive Interface Methodology Abstract Standard (PAIMAS), Personal ARchives Accessible in DIGital Media (PARADIGM), and Tufts Accessioning Program for Electronic Records (TAPER). PAIMAS provides guidance for developing processes for acquiring digital content from donors and informing the production of a well-formed SIP.[33] The goal of PAIMAS is to "identify, define and provide structure to the relationships and interactions between an information Producer and an Archive."[34] *Producer* is an OAIS term for donor or content creator. PAIMAS proposes that archives have formal requirements for transfer, in order to spell out what the donor provides during transfer and what the archives does, including requirements about donor agreements, metadata, and file formats. The goal of these requirements is to ensure that the terms are clearly understood by both donor and archives. While formal requirements may not be realistic for all archival institutions in all instances, PAIMAS can be used as aspirational guidance in developing transfer processes for born-digital content. For example, PAIMAS requirements could be turned into questions for donors during digital transfer and create guidance for revisions to deeds of gift that will contain born-digital materials. The National Archives (NARA) has recently published similar file format requirements for agencies transferring material to the archives.[35] The PARADIGM records survey, a series of questions related to records creation, use, formats, rights, and other topics, provides a model of a practical implementation of PAIMAS. Finally, Tufts University has systematized these ideas in TAPER.[36] TAPER uses Submission Agreement Forms and relevant

---

32 PARADIGM, "Working with Record Creators—Donation and Deposit Agreements," *Workbook on Digital Private Papers* (2005–2007), http://www.paradigm.ac.uk/workbook, captured at https://perma.cc/77FG-63QD.
33 Consultative Committee for Space Data Systems, *Producer Archive Interface Methodology Abstract Standard (PAIMAS)* (2004), http://public.ccsds.org/publications/archive/651x0m1.pdf, captured at https://perma.cc/PEV9-9DZ4.
34 PAIMAS, 1-1.
35 NARA bulletin 2014-04: Revised Format Guidance for the Transfer of Permanent Electronic Records (January 31, 2014), http://www.archives.gov/records-mgmt/bulletins/2014/2014-04.html, captured at https://perma.cc/KWP3-A2K6.
36 TAPER Project Deliverables website, http://sites.tufts.edu/dca/about-us/research-initiatives/taper-tufts-accessioning-program-for-electronic-records/deliverables/, captured at https://perma.cc/N8ZX-3BVA.

documentation (schemas, content models) to build an automated submission process. The output of the TAPER submission process is XML documentation of the submission agreement and context of records creation, both of which are important to the provenance thread of preservation metadata.

After reviewing some of the tools and workflows described in the resources above, archivists can create well-formed SIPs which translate to well-formed AIPs.

The Archival Information Package: What is an AIP?

SIPs are transformed into Archival Information Packages (AIPs) during the ingest process developed by the archives. Ingest is the process of transferring and validating the transfer of the SIP to archival storage. Depending on the systems in place, the ingest process may also generate additional metadata, such as checksums, file characterizations, and preservation event records, which will be incorporated into the AIP. Some ingest workflows may also involve file format migrations to create more sustainable and easily preservable objects within the AIP.

The AIP is the basis for many of the activities of a digital repository, including the generation of DIPs, or access packages. An AIP includes the digital object(s), metadata, and packaging necessary to preserve digital objects. This includes their context and any information necessary to **render** and access the files over time. More specifically, an AIP contains:

- Content: the information contained in the object (e.g., the contents of correspondence by an artist)
- Context: the information about the object (e.g., descriptive metadata, provenance information, documentation of actions performed on the object by the archives)
- Structure: the technical makeup of the object itself (e.g., file format, encryption information if files are encrypted, operating system used in creation)

An AIP is created through a set of processes performed on materials acquired by an archival repository. The SIP to AIP transformation is where the content, context, and structure of digital object(s) are documented and linked to the materials. Traditionally, archivists capture provenance information (who donated the materials, context of creation, and any preservation activities performed on the material by the archives). Similar actions are performed on digital objects, but instead of manual activities, software may be used to perform the preservation action and document the result.

When digital files are acquired, ideally they should be packaged by the donor in a digital container like a bag (created by BagIt or another packaging tool).[37] If files arrive without being packaged, the archives could do it after-the-fact (upon arrival). Ideally, items are packaged so that checksums can be generated and verified over time; this integrity checking starts at the time of acquisition. This can be compared to boxing up materials: it is hard to have physical and administrative control over papers that arrive loose or boxes that do not fit on the shelves.

If physical media is transferred, data should be copied from the media during acquisition by creating a **disk image**, or unaltered copies of the media contents. Disk images can be either **logical**, also called custom content images, copies of selected files, or **forensic**, bit-for-bit copies of the entire disk, including deleted files and unallocated space. Disk imaging requires special software (e.g., FTK Imager or Guymager) or a command line script that both creates and verifies an exact copy of the original data. Some disk imaging tool suites such as BitCurator and FTK include additional analysis tools (e.g., file type visualization, pattern recognition, metadata export) that can be helpful in both appraisal and processing. For more information on safely and consistently obtaining data from physical media, see the OCLC report, "You've Got to Walk Before You Can Run: First Steps for Managing Born-Digital Content Received on Physical Media," and BitCurator tool's documentation.[38]

More and more, digital objects are transferred over the network through services like Dropbox, Box, and Google Drive. With some of these transfer methods, you can confirm that you received exactly what the donor wished to transfer, down to the byte level. You can use tools like rsync, MD5Summer, or Exactly in some of these platforms.[39]

---

37 BagIt is a packaging specification hosted by Library of Congress, https://github.com/LibraryOfCongress/bagit-java, captured at https://perma.cc/9QPD-BKHW.
38 Erway, *You've Got to Walk Before You Can Run*.
39 MD5 Summer is a Windows application that generates and verifies MD5 checksums, available for download at http://linux.die.net/man/1/rsync, captured at https://perma.cc/9BKB-PU7S. See also http://www.md5summer.org/ (homepage captured at https://perma.cc/455L-ECZG) and https://www.avpreserve.com/tools/exactly/ (captured at https://perma.cc/2BH4-UC9H).

Having a consistent method for transfer—meaning a documented and repeatable process that uses a consistent set of tools with consistent outputs—leads to a more consistent package as a SIP. A well-formed SIP creates a better AIP. A consistent method can also create repeatable and measurable results so that an archives can perform quality assurance on their processes over time.

Preserving only the digital object or bytes and not the context or information about the structure of the object will create preservation issues in the future. Decades from now, archivists and users will need to know the technical characteristics of a file in order to make it meaningful and useable. How you implement this documentation for different formats and acquisitions is important. For emulation, an archivist or user would need to know the hardware and software needed to render the file in its original environment. For migration, the archivist or user would need to know about the structure of the object in order to determine a viable migration path (e.g., Rich Text Format to PDF). It is vital to determine what your repository will capture about digital objects—the data that forms your AIP. Creating a standardized way to do this through tools and technology builds consistent and more accurate AIPs.

In digital preservation terms, the AIP is the fundamental component within a digital repository. It contains the data and metadata that are used to generate a Dissemination Information Package (DIP) for access. Let's break down the AIP in OAIS terms to understand the technical pieces that form the archival package. For a more detailed breakdown of AIP elements, refer to the OCLC/RLG report on preservation metadata.[40]

1. *Content Information:* the content and structure of the AIP. The package that includes the bits of the object and the information that makes the bits renderable and interpretable.
    a) *Content Data Object:* the digital object itself.
    b) *Representation Information:* layers of information about the digital object that make it meaningful and interpretable.

---

40 OCLC/RLG Working Group on Preservation Metadata, "Preservation Metadata and the OAIS Information Model: A Metadata Framework to Support the Preservation of Digital Objects" (OCLC: June 2002), http://www.oclc.org/content/dam/research/activities/pmwg/pm_framework.pdf, captured at https://perma.cc/PL5J-TABH.

This information is captured in file format identification details, some of which can be generated by characterization software (file format encoding that is relevant to the designated community in order to make the digital object renderable). The two main components of representation information are:

    (1) *Structural Information:* data needed to represent the digital object from a technical perspective, such as the hardware and software needed to render the objects and the file formats within the AIP.

    (2) *Semantic Information:* data about how to represent the object from a content perspective, such as language of the text and any formal elements of the object.

2. *Preservation Description Information:* PDI is where the context surrounding the digital object is captured. The metadata that enables the long-term preservation of an AIP is broken down into four main areas:

    a) *Reference Information:* the assignment of **unique identification** of digital objects within the AIP, usually takes the form of a universally unique identifier (UUID).

    b) *Provenance Information:* custodial history of the digital objects in the AIP, including origination, as well as actions taken on the objects such as ingest, normalization, etc.

    c) *Context Information:* documents the relationship the digital objects have to other objects.

    d) *Fixity Information:* captures the action of validating the integrity of the digital objects (e.g., checksums).

3. *Packaging Information:* ties the digital objects and their associated metadata together as a unit.

4. *Descriptive Information:* usually pulled from content information and preservation, it is the subset of metadata used for discovery and access.

Having a clear, repeatable process for creating AIPs will ensure that digital objects are well documented, and can be monitored and assessed over time.

Well-formed AIPs should enable your organization to create well-formed Dissemination Information Packages (DIPs) for users

Preparing an Archival Information Package (AIP) for an Artist's Laptop

An archivist ingests the contents of a laptop from an artist. The archives decides to use a forensic capture approach and generates a disk image of the donated materials. Upon basic accession of the objects, the SIP would include:
- Forensic disk image of laptop contents
- High-level description of collection contents and custodial history (created by archivist or donor)
- Fixity information (checksums generated upon receipt for disk image)
- Any other requirements unique to the SIP specification

The archives will ingest the SIP into archival storage (either through a repository or manually). This process will include the activities necessary to create an AIP, including:
- Evaluating the disk image to ensure all the contents are in scope for acquisition
- Generating a universally unique identifier (UUID) for disk image
- Running checksums and evaluating against original checksums after files are moved to archival storage (verify fixity information)
- Using forensic tools to generate inventory; creating inventory of file and folder listing and exporting into METS structmap (structural listing of files and their hierarchy)
- Identifying event information
  - Software used to generate disk image
  - Who ingested materials (name of archivist or staff member)
  - When materials were ingested (timestamp)
  - File path of the destination path of the image after ingest
- Creating descriptive record about the digital objects, potentially captured from the export from the tools used to image and process the disk image (like DFXML), or created by documenting basic title, description, date, and creator fields
- Linking descriptive metadata and preservation metadata that is generated from tools to the content

For more detailed guidance on disk imaging, refer to Barrera-Gomez and Erway, *Walk This Way*.

For a more detailed example of implementation, see Chris Prom's blog post, "Archival Information Packet Structure," http://e-records.chrisprom.com/archival-information-packet-structure/, captured at https://perma.cc/GAT4-W2M9, and the Archivematica AIP structure, https://www.archivematica.org/wiki/AIP_structure, captured at https://perma.cc/N23Z-F82F.

requesting digital content. A DIP can contain one or more AIPs and is the package that is transmitted to a user to enable access and use of the digital objects in your custody. The OAIS Reference Model suggests DIPs be constructed based on designated communities' needs. For example, if you are collecting archaeological data and archaeologists are a designated community within your repository's user base, then you should build specifications for your DIPs that would enable the best possible use scenario for them. This may include specific descriptive metadata elements they use like archaeological site numbers or archaeological taxonomies, as well as access copies of digital objects in file formats that archaeologists use. As you can imagine, this type of information may change over time, so archives need to review their DIP specifications as new file formats and usage patterns evolve.

ISO 16363: A Related Standard for Trusted Digital Repositories

Using the OAIS Reference Model, ISO 16363 provides a set of organizational, technical, and business requirements for a trustworthy digital repository.[41] Auditors use ISO 16363 to assess whether a digital repository is trustworthy, but the document can also be used to do the reverse: inform requirements for the development of a system, with trustworthiness in mind.

Here are key characteristics for a trustworthy repository that you can start evaluating within your program as you build your digital preservation capabilities:

Organizational concerns
- Governance: Is there a group of stakeholders and framework in place to ensure the long-term preservation of these materials?
- Staffing: Are there sufficient staffing levels to ingest, describe, preserve, and provide access to these materials in your organization?
- Financial sustainability: Does the organization have committed funds to maintain current preservation levels and accommodate for additional growth in collections and processes? Is there a succession plan in place for your organization's holdings?
- Policy framework (policies and procedural accountability):

---

41 Consultative Committee for Space Data Systems, *Audit and Certification of Trustworthy Digital Repositories (ISO 16363)* (2011), http://public.ccsds.org/publications/archive/652x0m1.pdf, captured at https://perma.cc/8J63-TBEA.

Does your organization have a digital preservation policy that is in use, up-to-date, and has assigned responsibility to staff?
- Legal and contractual framework (the contracts, licenses, and liabilities under which the organization must operate): Does your organization have transfer agreements or deeds of gifts that allow for preservation actions to be taken on digital materials and clearly state when the repository takes on preservation responsibility for the objects?
- Digital object management: Are there good policies in place for how the repository receives SIPs, creates and manages AIPs and DIPs, and for how the repository documents its object management activities?

Technological concerns
- Hardware and software infrastructure: Does your organization have the hardware and software needed to manage objects?
- Data security: Does your organization have security and monitoring tools in place to protect data from alteration?

ISO 16363 chapters 3 (*Organizational Infrastructure*, which includes governance, financial accountability, and other programmatic elements) and 4 (*Digital Object Management*) can be mapped in a spreadsheet to use the standard as a requirements document for self-audit or for system selection.[42] Another document that can help inform the process is the TRAC Audit Checklist.[43] TRAC was developed in 2007 by OCLC's Research Libraries Group and the National Archives and Records Administration. ISO 16363 is largely based on the Trustworthy Digital Repository Checklist (TDR), part of TRAC. In Module 8, *Becoming a Trusted Digital Repository*, Steve Marks provides guidance for using the TRAC Audit Checklist to complete a self-audit and improve repository operations and trustworthiness based on the outcomes.[44] Self-certification, grounded in TRAC principles, is an

---

42 See Primary Trustworthy Digital Repository Authorisation Body (PTAB) website for an Excel spreadsheet template with these chapters' elements, http://www.iso16363.org/sdm_downloads/iso-16363-self-assessment-template/ spreadsheet, captured at https://perma.cc/ALW7-RB9L.
43 CRL, OCLC, Trustworthy Repositories Audit and Certification: Criteria and Checklist (2007), 53–73, http://www.crl.edu/sites/default/files/attachments/pages/trac_0.pdf, captured at https://perma.cc/8U6C-6MR2.
44 Steve Marks, *Module 8: Becoming a Trusted Digital Repository*, ed. Michael Shallcross (Chicago: Society of American Archivists, 2015).

emerging approach to demonstrating trustworthiness in a less costly and complex manner than the official certification. While TRAC or ISO 16363 certification is not necessary for all preservation environments, these documents can help institutions plan continuous improvement in digital preservation infrastructure, processes, and policies.

Preservation Actions in Context

The creation and long-term management of the AIP requires archivists to take a series of preservation actions. Preservation actions can be taken incrementally and/or iteratively as described in the National Digital Stewardship Alliance Levels of Preservation table.[45] This section will briefly review the most common types of preservation actions and their value to the longevity of the AIP.

Ingestion is often the first preservation action taken on an object; it signifies the transition from SIP to AIP. Ingestion connotes that the digital object has been transferred to its initial preservation storage environment. Usually this is a staging area where other preservation actions can be taken to prepare the AIP for its final preservation storage location, whether an institutional repository, digital preservation system, or secure file system storage.

Usually contemporaneous with ingest, *identifier assignment* is the process of associating AIPs with a consistent, persistent, and unique identifier. This is usually a UUID,[46] but it can also be a locally unique file name created according to institutional conventions. Identifiers are essential for object management within digital preservation systems, databases, or file systems.

Message digest calculation is "the process by which a message digest ('hash') is created."[47] The message digest, also known as a cryptographic hash value—or what we have called, up until now, a checksum—is the output, usually an alphanumeric string, of a mathematical algorithm which uses as its input a selection of bytes from a given file.

---

45 NDSA's Levels of Preservation, http://ndsa.diglib.org/activities/levels-of-digital-preservation/, captured at https://perma.cc/VY8Y-S3GU.
46 The Open Software Foundation developed a draft standard, now expired, for UUIDs. This draft continues to provide good guidance for the local development of identifier schemes. See http://www.opengroup.org/dce/info/draft-leach-uuids-guids-01.txt, captured at https://perma.cc/PZ89-WE22.
47 *PREMIS Data Dictionary for Preservation Metadata* version 2.2.

If a single byte is changed in the original file, the resulting message digest, or checksum, will also change. The generation of checksums is essential to managing object integrity over time. Through audits and *fixity checking*, "the process of verifying that an object has not been changed in a given period"—usually achieved by comparing checksums generated at ingest with those generated at various points after—archivists can attest to the integrity of their AIPs over time. If a fixity check reveals discrepancies in the digital objects' bit count between two copies, archivists can identify intentional or accidental alterations or degradation.[48]

When ingesting new objects archivists should strongly consider placing them in *quarantine*, a location where new files are segregated (i.e., non-networked) from "clean" objects already in preservation storage. Quarantine prevents viruses or malware potentially present in new acquisitions from infecting or altering other objects. Create a process where incoming digital objects remain in quarantine until virus definitions will catch up with any new malware. Upon successful completion of a *virus check*, "the process of scanning a file for malicious programs," new objects can be removed from quarantine or *unquarantined*.[49]

Format identification is the determination of file format. This can be accomplished through examination of file extension, file structure, or comparison with format registries, which are compendiums (databases) of information about file formats such as their versions, names, extensions, and related software. PRONOM, developed by the National Archives of the United Kingdom, is a notable example of a file format registry.[50] Format identification informs decisions related to normalization and migration or emulation. Once a format is identified, *validation*—"the process of comparing an object with a standard and noting compliance or exceptions"—can determine well-formedness, which is essential for rendering a digital object via computer software so that the object can be interpreted by humans.[51]

Replication is "the process of creating a copy of an object that is, bit-wise, identical to the original."[52] Replication and redundancy are

---

48   Ibid.
49   Ibid., 135.
50   PRONOM: The technical registry, http://apps.nationalarchives.gov.uk/PRONOM/Default.aspx, captured at https://perma.cc/D7P4-HKQ2.
51   *PREMIS Data Dictionary for Preservation Metadata* version 2.2.
52   Ibid., 134–135.

essential to mitigate risks to the object such as alteration, corruption, degradation, or natural disaster. Maintaining and managing multiple copies of objects, ideally in different physical locations, lessens the risk that content will be irreparably lost. Archives can do this by configuring their preservation storage to have at least three copies, on diverse storage media, housed in at least two distinct geographic locations.

Related to format identification and validation, *normalization* is transformation of an object to conform with a standard predetermined format, intended to create a version that is more sustainable or easier for users to render and view. Factors that increase the sustainability of a format are the availability of well-documented specifications, wide adoption of the format for use, and few external dependencies that would inhibit migration or inspection. For example, an institution may decide to normalize all incoming graphic files (e.g., BMP, JPEG) to TIFF. Along the same lines, *migration* is "a transformation of an object creating a version in a more contemporary format."[53] For example, an institution may decide to migrate a Word document created using Microsoft Word '97 to a version such as Microsoft Word 2013, by opening and resaving the document in a more recent version of the program. Both of these transformational actions are optional and wholly dependent on projected access. When considering either action, archivists should take into account the target user communities and their needs. The significant properties of a particular format can also inform these decisions.[54]

Preservation actions lend themselves to systematic processes, tools, and automation. Details and comparisons of these tools can be found below.

Digital Object Description and Management

Digital object description and management tools and systems are widely used in the archival community. These systems can facilitate use and access and provide descriptive and contextual linking between objects, but they do not always provide for storage of preservation metadata and contextual information. Some institutions utilize

---

53 Ibid.
54 The properties of a document must be maintained in order for the content of the document to persist (e.g., a color drawing of a rainbow must retain its color and orientation of lines in order to be recognizable as a rainbow).

multiple connected systems to manage various facets of preservation, description, and access to their collections.

Digital Preservation Systems (DPS) are commonly large, workflow-driven systems that allow for ingest, analysis, processing, and auditing of digital objects. Some allow for application and storage of descriptive metadata. All should manage and generate administrative and technical metadata surrounding the preservation of digital objects.

Collections Management Systems (CMS) are generally database applications intended to maintain descriptive and sometimes administrative information about physical and digital collections including records of provenance, acquisition, archival description, and rights and location management. Some administrative metadata relevant to digital preservation can be stored in a collections management database. Some collections management systems allow for storage of digital surrogates for the purposes of access and management of collections, not for digital preservation.

Institutional Repositories (IR) are systems implemented to manage and provide access to digital works. Materials may include scholarly works such as publications, open access journals, and digitized materials. IRs are geared more toward open access to individual items such as publications, as opposed to preservation of aggregate materials like archival collections.

Digital Asset Management Systems (DAMS) are systems to store, describe, and retrieve digital materials. DAMS often include photographic assets, including born-digital and digitized images. DAMS are often primarily access and dissemination platforms, with limited preservation or management functions.

Not all of these types of systems are built or designed to perform digital preservation functions, but many libraries and archives use these types of systems to manage digital objects. It is important to understand how these systems function within your institution and how they can help you achieve your digital preservation goals. The following table compares some common tools and systems in terms of their ability to perform certain preservation functions.

Figure 2. Tool Comparison Table

	Generates METS	Processes METS structmap and maintains relationships between objects	Generates PREMIS	Generates MODS
DIGITAL PRESERVATION SYSTEM				
Archivematica	X	X	X	X
Preservica		X	Generates something similar	
Rosetta		X	X	
Fedora/Hydra	X	X	X	X
COLLECTIONS MANAGEMENT SYSTEMS				
Archivists' Toolkit	Can export METS			Can export MODS
Archon				
ArchivesSpace	Can export METS	Can import METS	Might be able to export PREMIS in future	Can export MODS
ICA AtoM		Can import METS	X	X
INSTITUTIONAL REPOSITORIES				
DSpace	Can export METS	Can import METS	Can import/export PREMIS	Can import/export MODS
EPrints	Can export METS			Can export MODS
Greenstone	X	X		
Digital Commons				
Fedora/Hydra	X	X	X	X
DIGITAL ASSET MANAGEMENT SYSTEMS				
Content DM	X			
Digitool	X	X	X	
ResourceSpace				

Preserving Digital Objects   35

Generates and records checksums	Generates unique IDs	Performs file format ID	Performs file format normalization	Has API	Manages descriptive metadata
X	X	X	X	X	X
X	X	X	X	X	X
X	X	X	X	X	X
X	X	X	X	X	X
				X	X
				X	X
	X			X	X
					X
X	X			X	X
X	X	X		X	X
	X			X	X
	X				X
X	X	X	X	X	X
	X			X	X
	X			X	X
	X	X		X	X

Other Tools

In filling out preservation workflows, some institutions may take advantage of function-specific tools that complement their in-place systems.

SIP and AIP preparation tools include:

- BagIt, https://github.com/LibraryOfCongress/bagit-java. Open source packaging format for materials to facilitate transfer and validation of transfer when acquiring data from donors or moving it between systems (e.g., ingest). Creates checksums and other integrity-checking features for the bag and individual set of objects.
- BitCurator, http://www.bitcurator.net/. A set of open source tools specifically packaged for libraries and archives to use when applying forensic techniques to digital acquisitions and processing. This tool can be used to prepare AIPs when using a disk imaging technique for incoming materials.
- Curator's Workbench, http://blogs.lib.unc.edu/cdr/index.php/about-the-curators-workbench/. Digital acquisitions and processing tool. Performs automated staging of incoming content, including checksums, UUID generation, and METS **structmap** of file list. The tool has a built-in MODS editor that allows for the application of descriptive metadata to objects. You can arrange files and folders and deselect items (appraise out) before preparing the AIP for storage.
- Data Accessioner, http://dataaccessioner.org/. Tool to enable digital transfer and validation. Tool enables transfer of content to archival storage and performs checksums, extracts technical metadata via FITS, and compiles an XML output from the process.
- Exactly, https://www.avpreserve.com/tools/exactly/. A tool based on BagIt specifications that enables digital transfer and validation. Tool enables transfer of content via Secure File Transfer Protocol (SFTP) or other networked locations, validates bag content, validates content after transfer, and allows for custom metadata generation and email notification when transfer is complete.
- Fixity, https://www.avpreserve.com/tools/fixity/. Tool to perform checksum calculation and analysis over a set of files.

Reports can be sent to archivists after fixity analysis is complete and indicate where any issue with file integrity is identified.
- NARA File Analyzer, https://github.com/usnationalarchives/File-Analyzer. Tool that performs fixity and quality control analysis over files. Could be used as part of SIP to AIP transformation or across files staged for ingest.

File format identification tools help provide a component of the representation information of the AIP.
- DROID, http://www.nationalarchives.gov.uk/information-management/projects-and-work/droid.htm
- PRONOM, http://www.nationalarchives.gov.uk/aboutapps/pronom/
- File Information Tool Set (FITS), http://projects.iq.harvard.edu/fits
- Unified Digital Format Registry (UDFR), http://www.udfr.org/

Tools for audio-visual resources include:
- FADGI, http://www.digitizationguidelines.gov/, Federal Agencies Digitization Guidelines Initiative. Provides a suite of guidelines for digitization and reproduction efforts.
- EXIFtool, http://www.sno.phy.queensu.ca/~phil/exiftool/. A command line tool to extract, edit, and review metadata from a variety of file formats, including digital image formats.
- FFmpeg, http://www.ffmpeg.org/about.html. Toolsuite to decode, transcode, or play audio or video files.

Summary and Recommendations

As we have seen in the preceding sections, preserving digital objects is a critical and complex endeavor. Digital objects and their metadata can be acquired, created, combined, and managed in various ways. The case studies in Appendix B show how two institutions have designed and implemented their preservation workflows, balancing best practices with local requirements. The cases studies demonstrate how different archives grapple with complex problems, and make decisions to address them.

The following practices will help other archives to likewise enable the long-term sustainability of their digital objects:

- Identifying the components that contribute to preservability of objects, such as metadata about the file formats, context of creation, and preservation actions taken
- Understanding core principles, practices, and standards, from both the archival and digital preservation community
- Researching the particular tools and systems available to facilitate metadata creation, preservation activities, and management of objects
- Developing and documenting local implementation of standards and processes for acquiring, packaging, ingesting, managing, migrating, and monitoring preservation objects
- Projecting and planning preservation improvements, adding incrementally to capabilities
- Evaluating and auditing the health of digital objects and the systems that hold them

All archives need to be prepared to steward the digital objects in their care into the future and ensure their long-term accessibility. Using the information in this module and the further readings as a starting point, archives and archivists responsible for digital collections can take steps to reach these goals.

Appendix A: Further Readings

AIMS Work Group. AIMS Born-Digital Collections: An Inter-Institutional Model for Stewardship. University of Virginia Library, 2012. http://dcs.library.virginia.edu/aims/white-paper/. Captured at https://perma.cc/9E3J-8SCH.

Barrera-Gomez, Julianna, and Ricky Erway. *Walk This Way: Detailed Steps for Transferring Born-Digital Content from Media You Can Read In-house.* Dublin, OH: OCLC Research, 2013. http://www.oclc.org/content/dam/research/publications/library/2013/2013-02.pdf. Captured at https://perma.cc/VX9C-LJ59.

British Library. British Library Digital Preservation Strategy. London, 2013. http://www.bl.uk/aboutus/stratpolprog/collectioncare/digitalpreservation/strategy/BLDigitalPreservationStrategy_2013-16-external.pdf. Captured at https://perma.cc/U89H-2APP.

Consultative Committee for Space Data Systems. *Audit and Certification of Trustworthy Digital Repositories.* Washington, DC, 2011. http://public.ccsds.org/publications/archive/652x0m1.pdf. Captured at https://perma.cc/8J63-TBEA.

Consultative Committee for Space Data Systems. *Reference Model for an Open Archival Information System (OAIS).* Washington, DC, 2012. http://public.ccsds.org/publications/archive/650x0m2.pdf. Captured at https://perma.cc/4C6D-BAJA.

CRL and OCLC. Trustworthy Repositories Audit and Certification: Criteria and Checklist. http://www.crl.edu/sites/default/files/attachments/pages/trac_0.pdf. Captured at https://perma.cc/8U6C-6MR2.

Daines, J. Gordon. "Module 2: Processing Digital Records and Manuscripts." In *Archival Arrangement and Description*, edited by Christopher J. Prom and Thomas J. Frusciano. Chicago: Society of American Archivists, 2012.

Digital Creation and Preservation Working Group. UMass Amherst Libraries Digital Preservation Policy. Amherst, 2011. http://www.library.umass.edu/assets/aboutus/attachments/University-of-Massachusetts-Amherst-Libraries-Digital-Preservation-Policy3-18-2011-templated.pdf. Captured at https://perma.cc/D6SL-GMKT.

Duranti, Luciana. "Reliability and Authenticity: The Concepts and Their Implications." *Archivaria* 39 (1995): 5–10. http://journals.sfu.ca/archivar/index.php/archivaria/article/viewFile/12063/13035. Captured at https://perma.cc/494J-S649.

Eastwood, Terry, Bart Ballaux, Rachel Mills, and Randy Preston. "Appendix 14: Chain of Preservation Model—Diagrams and Definitions." *International Research on Permanent Authentic Records in Electronic Systems (InterPARES) 2: Experiential, Interactive and Dynamic Records,* edited by Luciana Duranti and Randy Preston. Rome: Associazione Nazionale Archivistica Italiana, 2008. http://www.interpares.org/display_file.cfm?doc=ip2_book_appendix_14.pdf. Captured at https://perma.cc/AQ9K-CU7B.

Erway, Ricky. *Swatting the Long Tail of Digital Media: A Call for Collaboration.* Dublin, OH: OCLC Research, 2012. http://www.oclc.org/content/dam/research/publications/library/2012/2012-08.pdf. Captured at https://perma.cc/LKW8-N9EA.

Forstrom, Michael. "Managing Electronic Records in Manuscript Collections: A Case Study from the Beinecke Rare Book and Manuscript Library." *The American Archivist* 72 (2009): 460–477. doi: http://dx.doi.org/10.17723/aarc.72.2.b82533tvr7713471.

Gengenbach, Martin. "'The Way We Do It Here': Mapping Digital Forensics Workflows in Collecting Institutions." Master's Paper for the M.S. in L.S. degree, University of North Carolina at Chapel Hill, 2012. http://digitalcurationexchange.org/system/files/gengenbach-forensic-workflows-2012.pdf. Captured at https://perma.cc/V4HE-SCJC.

Harvey, Ross. *Digital Curation: A How-To-Do-It Manual.* New York: Neal-Schuman Publishers, 2004.

Hedstrom, Margaret. "Digital Preservation: A Time Bomb for Digital Libraries." *Computers and the Humanities* 31 (1998): 195–196. http://deepblue.lib.umich.edu/bitstream/handle/2027.42/42573/?sequence=1.

Heslop, H., S. Davis, and A. Wilson. *An Approach to the Preservation of Digital Records.* Canberra: National Archives of Australia, 2002.

International Research on Permanent Authentic Records in Electronic Systems (InterPARES) 2: Experiential, Interactive and Dynamic Records. "Creator Guidelines: Making and Maintaining Digital Materials: Guidelines for Individuals." http://www.interpares.org/public_documents/ip2(pub)preserver_guidelines_booklet.pdf. Captured at https://perma.cc/DD46-27P8.

John, Jeremy Leighton. "Digital Forensics and Preservation." DPC Technology Watch Report 12-03. Digital Preservation Coalition, 2012. http://dx.doi.org/10.7207/twr12-03.

Kott, Katherine, and Tom Cramer. "Designing and Implementing Second Generation Digital Preservation Services: A Scalable Model for the Stanford Digital Repository." *D-Lib Magazine* 16, no. 9/10 (2010). http://www.dlib.org/dlib/september10/cramer/09cramer.html. Captured at https://perma.cc/46A6-MEFH.

Lavoie, Brian, and Richard Gartner. "Preservation Metadata (2nd edition)." DPC Technology Watch Report 13-03. Digital Preservation Coalition, May 2013. doi: http://dx.doi.org/10.7207/twr13-03.

McDonald, John. "Managing Records in the Modern Office: Taming the Wild Frontier." *Archivaria* 39 (1995): 70–79. http://journals.sfu.ca/archivar/index.php/archivaria/article/download/12069/13047. Captured at https://perma.cc/GJZ7-SQ4Z.

Marks, Steve. *Module 8: Becoming a Trusted Digital Repository.* Edited by Michael Shallcross. Chicago: Society of American Archivists, 2015.

NARA Bulletin 2014-04: Revised Format Guidance for the Transfer of Permanent Electronic Records. January 31, 2014. http://www.archives.gov/records-mgmt/bulletins/2014/2014-04.html. Captured at https://perma.cc/KWP3-A2K6.

NDSA Levels of Preservation. http://ndsa.diglib.org/activities/levels-of-digital-preservation/. Captured at https://perma.cc/VY8Y-S3GU.

O'Meara, Erin, and Meg Tuomala. "Finding Balance Between Archival Principles and Real-Life Practices in an Institutional Repository." *Archivaria* 73 (2012): 81–103. http://journals.sfu.ca/archivar/index.php/archivaria/article/view/13385/14693. Captured at https://perma.cc/GUB3-CK9T.

OCLC/RLG Working Group on Preservation Metadata. "Preservation Metadata and the OAIS Information Model: A Metadata Framework to Support the Preservation of Digital Objects." OCLC, June 2002. http://www.oclc.org/content/dam/research/activities/pmwg/pm_framework.pdf. Captured at https://perma.cc/PL5J-TABH.

Onuf, Rachel, and Tom Hyry. "Take It Personally: The Implications of Personal Records in Electronic Form." In *I, Digital: Personal Collections in the Digital Era*, edited by Christopher A. Lee. Chicago: Society of American Archivists, 2011.

PARADIGM. "Project Overview." Last modified February 18, 2008. http://www.paradigm.ac.uk/about/index.html. Captured at http://www.webarchive.org.uk/wayback/archive/20081001093108/http://www.paradigm.ac.uk/workbook/pdfs/index.htm.

Pearce-Moses, Richard. "Janus in Cyberspace: Archives on the Threshold of the Digital Era." *The American Archivist* 70 (2007): 13–22. http://dx.doi.org/10.17723/aarc.70.1.n7121165223j6t83.

PREMIS Editorial Committee. *PREMIS Data Dictionary for Preservation Metadata* version 2.2. July 2012: 134. http://www.loc.gov/standards/premis/v2/premis-2-2.pdf. Captured at https://perma.cc/2WSX-4WRC.

PREMIS Editorial Committee. "Guidelines for using PREMIS with METS for Exchange." Revised September 17, 2008. http://www.loc.gov/standards/premis/guidelines-premismets.pdf. Captured at https://perma.cc/7DMD-B3KF.

Prom, Christopher. "Preserving Email." DPC Technology Watch Report 11-01. Digital Preservation Coalition, December 2011. doi: http://dx.doi.org/10.7207/twr11-01.

Redwine, Gabriela, et al. *Born Digital: Guidance for Donors, Dealers, and Archival Repositories*. CLIR Publication 159. Washington, DC: Council on Library and Information Resources, 2013. http://www.clir.org/pubs/reports/pub159/pub159.pdf. Captured at https://perma.cc/4BN3-6XJG.

Rimkus, Kyle. "Digital Preservation File Format Policies of ARL Member Libraries: An Analysis." *D-Lib Magazine* 20, no. 3/4 (2014). http://www.dlib.org/dlib/march14/rimkus/03rimkus.html. Captured at https://perma.cc/4BN3-6XJG.

Rothenberg, Jeff. "Ensuring the Longevity of Digital Documents." *Scientific American* 272, no. 1 (1995): 24–29. http://www.scientificamerican.com/article/ensuring-the-longevity-of-digital-d/. Captured at https://perma.cc/UE2U-MFS3.

Shallcross, Michael, and Nancy Deromedi. "Automating Digital Processing at the Bentley Historical Society." Poster, paper, and slides, 2012. http://deepblue.lib.umich.edu/handle/2027.42/95923.

Sheldon, Madeline. *An Analysis of Current Digital Preservation Policies: Archives, Libraries, and Museums.* 2013. http://www.digitalpreservation.gov/documents/Analysis%20of%20Current%20Digital%20Preservation%20Policies.pdf. Captured at https://perma.cc/4Q6X-XJZA.

Sierman, Barbara, Catherine Jones, Sean Bechhofer, and Gry Elstrom, "Preservation Policy Levels in SCAPE." In *iPRES 2013: Proceedings of the 10th International Conference on Preservation of Digital Objects*, edited by José Borbinha, Michael Nelson, and Steve Knight. http://purl.pt/24107/1/iPres2013_PDF/Preservation%20Policy%20Levels%20in%20SCAPE.pdf. Captured at https://perma.cc/FHQ7-5XR9.

Tanner, Simon. *Measuring the Impact of Digital Resources: The Balanced Value Impact Model.* London: King's College, October 2012. www.kdcs.kcl.ac.uk/innovation/impact.html. Captured at https://perma.cc/Z2RR-K6NS.

Thinking Records, James Lappin's blog on records management and electronic records. http://thinkingrecords.co.uk/.

Thomas, Susan. "Curating the I, Digital: Experiences at the Bodleian Library." In *I, Digital: Personal Collections in the Digital Era*, edited by Christopher A. Lee. Chicago: Society of American Archivists, 2011.

Weldon, Edward. "Archives and the Challenges of Change." *The American Archivist* 46, no. 2 (1983): 125–134. doi: http://dx.doi.org/10.17723/aarc.46.2.g91733970404m01p.

Appendix B: Case Studies

Case Study 1: Rockefeller Archive Center

By Sibyl Schaefer, former Assistant Director, Head of Digital Programs

Please provide a brief description of your organization (or library or archives within the organization) and a brief description of the digital preservation program/repository (team composition, systems, tools, and infrastructure).

The Rockefeller Archive Center (RAC) is an independent repository and research center dedicated to the study of philanthropy and the diverse domains shaped by philanthropy. It was established in 1974 to assemble, preserve, and make accessible the records of the Rockefeller family and their wide-ranging philanthropic endeavors (including the Rockefeller Foundation, the Rockefeller Brothers Fund, and the Rockefeller University). Today, the Center's growing holdings include materials from numerous non-Rockefeller foundations and nonprofit organizations, making it a premier center for research on philanthropy and civil society. It is also a major repository for the personal papers of leaders of the philanthropic community, Nobel Prize laureates, and world-renowned investigators in science and medicine.

The archives side of the RAC consists of five main areas: donor relations and collection development, reference, processing, archival services, and digital programs. The digital programs team consists of four full-time employees (one assistant director, one archivist, and two assistant archivists) and is responsible for maintaining and developing online access tools, digitization, archival technology support, and digital preservation. Although responsibilities vary from team member to team member, in general there are about 1.5 full-time employees dedicated to digital preservation tasks.

We use a variety of systems and tools to aid our digital preservation work. We have purchased a Forensic Recovery of Evidence Device (FRED)[55] and use that, as well as a Device Side Data FC5025[56] to image

---

[55] http://www.digitalintelligence.com/products/fred/, captured at https://perma.cc/49CX-TXZC.
[56] http://www.deviceside.com/fc5025.html, captured at https://perma.cc/KU4N-AU42.

digital media. We are in the process of purchasing a Kryoflux[57] for imaging as well.

We use Archivematica to ingest and package our AIPs. Our main AIPstore is file system based (not a repository like DSpace or Fedora). It is backed up to tape regularly, and we are planning on storing tapes offsite in a newly built storage facility. We check the fixity of the AIPs at regular intervals using the Ace Audit Manager.[58] We are also currently in the process of joining the MetaArchive[59] network to store selected AIPs in a LOCKSS[60] system. We initially made the decision not to adopt a repository system because we couldn't afford the technical expertise required. Since then, our in-house technical expertise has been expanded and the expertise required has been lowered by systems like Hydra[61] and Islandora,[62] so we may revisit that decision in the future.

Walk us through your ingest and AIP creation workflow.

In general, after we receive a data transfer or image a disk, we run virus checks, extract the directory structure of the disk image or data transfer, generate checksums, and then move the data to a staging server. A staging server is a separate area where we store data while preparing it for archival storage. Some of the data we receive from donors is transferred in bags,[63] in which case we leave them as bags for ingest. Prior to ingest, we assess any access or use restrictions that pertain to the materials. We try to do this at the largest aggregation possible, and if necessary, divide aggregations up by their restrictions.

Our ingest method follows the Archivematica ingest workflow, which processes materials through a series of microservices: file format identification, assignment of unique identifiers, metadata extraction, etc. We review rights and restrictions for the materials so we can enter PREMIS information during ingest. During this process, Archivematica packages the ingest into a bag (if it's not already bagged)

---

57 http://www.kryoflux.com/, captured at https://perma.cc/V9MN-2MDN.
58 https://wiki.umiacs.umd.edu/adapt/index.php/Ace:Main, captured at https://perma.cc/J3RT-XKBK.
59 http://www.metaarchive.org/, captured at https://perma.cc/36Y7-HQSB.
60 http://www.lockss.org/, captured at https://perma.cc/RE25-XXFN.
61 http://projecthydra.org/, captured at https://perma.cc/P9ZH-D3F7.
62 http://islandora.ca/, captured at https://perma.cc/T488-4WXH.
63 https://github.com/LibraryOfCongress/bagit-java, captured at https://perma.cc/9QPD-BKHW.

and generates an AIP that includes the standard bag manifest files, as well as log files generated during the virus scan and file format identification processes, any metadata that was submitted with the package, any additional submission documentation, the actual objects themselves (and normalized versions, if those were created), and a METS file containing the structure of the objects and PREMIS events, agents, and rights information. See the Archivematica wiki for a more detailed description of workflow elements.[64]

At the end of ingest, the AIP is stored on our Isilon storage server[65] and a DIP is generated. We have connected Archivematica with our Archivists' Toolkit (AT) database so that we can match digital objects with their corresponding AT components, and automatically generate AT digital object records with the correct rights and restrictions information.

As mentioned earlier, selected AIPs will be copied on to a different server in order for the MetaArchive crawler to ingest them into the MetaArchive LOCKSS system. Costs for this service are not insignificant, so we have decided to submit only materials in which the digital version is considered the preservation copy. For example, we have terabytes of digitized microfilm. Because we consider the microfilm to be the preservation copy, we will not ingest that data into MetaArchive.

Currently we are only packaging digital objects that have been processed through Archivematica. We're planning on using the backlog function in Archivematica for unprocessed materials so we can manage them in the same system and identify any necessary preservation issues.

Provide a generic or specific example of an AIP (in a diagram or schema). How does your AIP represent or account for the three main elements described in Lavoie and Gartner's diagram?

- **content information**
- **preservation description information**
- **packaging information**[66]

---

64 https://www.archivematica.org/wiki/AIP_structure, captured at https://perma.cc/A98G-T2WB.
65 Isilon is a networked attached storage server sold by EMC.
66 Brian Lavoie and Richard Gartner, "Preservation Metadata (2nd edition)," DPC Technology Watch Report 13-03 (Digital Preservation Coalition, May 2013), 14. doi: http://dx.doi.org/10.7207/twr13-03.

The Archivematica wiki shows how our AIPs are structured:

Content information

- *Content data object*: Original objects stored in the data/objects directory
- *Representation information*: File format identifiers are captured using FIDO[67] during ingest and recorded in the METS/PREMIS file. The appropriate PRONOM IDs are also stored.

Preservation Description Information

- *Reference:* Archivematica assigns UUIDs to each object in the ingest, as well as the ingest itself. These are all listed/organized in the METS <structmap>.
- *Context*: Relationships are also listed in the METS <structmap>. We have also added some complexity to this information by altering our data ingest structure when several digitized images comprise one PDF, so that the master TIFFs, adjusted JPEGs, and access PDFs are all related correctly. We are looking forward to the Yale-sponsored Archivematica development allowing ingest of disk images, in the hope that it will extract filesystem information automatically.
- *Provenance information*: This is probably a weak spot for us, because the finding aid in AT has the authoritative version of this information. I have debated including a finding aid in the submission documentation, but our ingests are often broken up into groupings smaller than the collection level, so we would have to ingest the same finding aid numerous times. This is not a big deal for small finding aids, but some of our finding aids are quite large. We are titling the ingests by the unique finding aid ID so there is some link between the two.
- *Fixity information*: This information is auto-generated by Archivematica and stored in the METS file as well as the BagIt manifests.

---

67 https://github.com/openplanets/fido, captured at https://perma.cc/JM6C-WUXN.

Packaging Information

The Archivematica files we generate cover the major packaging information reflected in the Lavoie and Gartner publication, the weak spot being the descriptive metadata, which is captured in the AT. We are looking to integrate our descriptive information more. We have done the first step—connecting our archival data system (the Archivists' Toolkit) with Archivematica to ensure that object UUIDs are linked and recorded in the AT. The next step is to do the reverse: record descriptive information currently in the AT in the AIP. Archivematica does provide for descriptive metadata ingest, but it is based on Dublin Core, and all our descriptive data is in EAD, so there are hierarchical data mapping issues to resolve. We've held off delving into this because we're planning on migrating to ArchivesSpace and potentially adopting systems like Islandora or Hydra, both of which are being integrated with Archivematica and may alleviate this gap.

One area we would like to improve is the recording of preservation actions taken prior to ingest. So, if we imaged a disk, we want to document what software and hardware we used to create the disk image, or if we extracted files from an image, etc. We currently record this type of information in a separate database, but ideally it would be stored in the METS/PREMIS record.

How do you perform preservation management activities on these objects? Specifically, how do you ensure the integrity of the objects in your care?

If needed, files are normalized during ingest. We store one copy of the AIP in our AIPstore and run regular fixity checks on them. In the very near future, some of our AIPs will also be ingested into MetaArchive for geographic redundancy as well as regular fixity verification. We still have a lot of work to do as far as disk imaging, description, etc., but once we have those priorities worked out, the plan is to create file format audits to identify at-risk formats. Because our ingests have been only of digitized items, I am comfortable holding off on this. The priority now is to get data off of obsolete media and migrate those files as needed (or desired).

What are some of the challenges you face preserving digital objects? What are some next steps and new features you want to add to your digital preservation program?

Our biggest challenge is simply being a small team with big goals. Prioritizing those goals is essential, but it also means we have a list of tasks we know we have to address but cannot currently commit to. Our main focus now is surveying collections for digital media and then imaging that media. At the same time, we are setting up workflows for the transfer and ingest of electronic records received from donors, and also processing and describing electronic records. We also are trying to integrate the management of digital records throughout the archives, so that those currently accessioning paper records will be accessioning digital, those processing paper will process digital, etc. Incorporating digital workflows will require training across other units in the archive, especially with the addition of new tools and software for staff to use.

My next steps are to continue to automate tasks, provide different levels of access within the same system (for donors, for archivists, for researchers), manage descriptive data more effectively, and develop workflows for disk image ingest. As mentioned earlier, we plan on reviewing repository systems like Islandora and Hydra, probably within the next two years.

What do you look for when evaluating tools and developing workflows for preserving digital objects? What type of requirements are essential to achieve your goals?

We are very much an open source shop and try to implement open source tools and solutions whenever possible. I feel the transparency of open source programs is essential in long-term digital preservation. I also look for the widespread adoption of a program or tool, sponsorship by a notable organization, and fairly recent development work done on it. BagIt is a good example of both of those—widely used (enough that we can request bags from vendors) and sponsored by the Library of Congress. Documentation of the tool—how it works as well as how to use it—is also important. Tools that archivists outside of the digital team will be using have to be user-friendly. This is a big reason that I decided to use FTK for processing rather than other open source options.

As far as developing workflows, I aim for automation of repetitive tasks, simplicity, and ease of use.

Do you have any advice for repositories just starting out in digital preservation? What are some of the first steps that someone could take?

I have to agree with the OCLC reports on getting started with born-digital materials:[68] the first step should be to identify and separate digital media from your collections (creating separation documentation, of course), and then get that data (preferably as disk images) onto a backed-up server. Next steps include virus checks, the creation of fixity information, and file format identification. Reviewing the results of those three activities should give you an idea of the potential value of the material as well as potential risks and/or preservation issues.

One thing I strongly advise against is simply adopting some sort of preservation system right off the bat. Preservation is a core archival function, and I really worry that institutions that contract with these types of services are simply handing it off instead of building long-term institutional knowledge and policies on how to manage digital materials. I am constantly reviewing our tech support's decisions to see if they make sense from an archival standpoint, and I find things that need modification all the time. For example, the Linux arguments used when mounting a disk for virus checking—I had numerous arguments that I added in order to ensure the integrity of the data was protected. I have the ability to do this because I can access these commands in my workflow or in my systems. How does that work when the system is closed? And what happens when no one is responsible for building the knowledge within the institution to ask that type of question?

---

68 Demystifying Born Digital series, http://oclc.org/research/activities/borndigital.html, captured at https://perma.cc/K27D-9FCN.

Case Study 2: University of North Carolina–Chapel Hill

By Jill Sexton, former Head of Digital Research Services; Meg Tuomala, former Electronic Records Archivist; and Gregory Jansen, former Lead Repository Developer

Please provide a brief description of your organization (or library or archives within the organization) and a brief description of the digital preservation program/repository (team composition, systems, tools, and infrastructure).

The University of North Carolina at Chapel Hill is a public university supporting 78 bachelor's, 112 master's, 68 doctorate, and seven professional degree programs through 14 schools and the College of Arts and Sciences. More than 29,000 undergraduate, graduate, and professional students learn from a faculty of 3,600. UNC Chapel Hill Libraries is a large research library with a staff of around 300, and collections of 7.4 million volumes, 4.5 million microforms, and 25 million manuscripts.

At UNC Libraries, digital preservation efforts are coordinated by the Digital Preservation and Stewardship Committee, whose charge is to align information and activities related to all aspects of digital preservation, for example, the creation and review of policy documents, the management of perpetual access files for licensed content, and the creation of guidelines for donors and collectors of digital content. Furthermore, these efforts are distributed across several library departments including Library and Information Technology, University Archives and Records Management Services, the Wilson Special Collections Library, and Library Preservation.

Development of a preservation repository was an early priority for UNC Libraries. Starting in 2006, the Library collaborated with campus partners, especially faculty and graduate students from UNC Chapel Hill's School of Information and Library Science, to develop specifications for the new repository. Software development began in 2008, and in 2010 the Carolina Digital Repository (CDR) began accepting submissions. The repository accepts born-digital special collections, digital research data collections and other scholarly output, and digitized library materials.

Digital Repository Services is a sub-unit under Library and Information Technology, and is fortunate to have a unit of four full-time staff dedicated to the development of the CDR.[69] Staff from Digital Repository Services in the Library and Information Technology department work closely with archivists from University Archives and Records Management Services and Special Collections Technical Services to determine requirements for system functionality, set enhancement priorities, and move materials into our preservation environment.

Following standards developed in the reference model for Open Archival Information Systems (OAIS), the CDR uses the Fedora Commons Repository as an object, model, and services provider and iRODS as a distributed storage and preservation system. We use a locally developed tool, the Curator's Workbench,[70] to facilitate the management, staging, description, and ingest of large batches of objects destined for the CDR.

The CDR also supports other means of ingest, such as automated ingest of content from aggregators via SWORD, and patron-initiated ingest of materials such as ETDs and research posters, via web forms. We offer a range of access controls based on campus LDAP[71] groups, which allow us to specify embargoes and access controls at the data stream level to any object in the repository.

Walk us through your ingest and AIP creation workflow.

Our high-level process is:

Submission preparation tool (Curator's Workbench and others)

Submission service (Admin web application)

- Validation (persistence module)
- Transformation to ingest batch (persistence module)
- Routine pre-processing of ingest batch (persistence module)
- Queues ingest batch with Fedora ingest service

Fedora ingest service

- First come, first served batch ingest
- Handling of diverse SOAP faults, protocol and service exceptions

---

69 https://cdr.lib.unc.edu/, captured at https://perma.cc/7V9K-KTBG.
70 https://github.com/UNC-Libraries/Curators-Workbench, captured at https://perma.cc/H79H-4YM4.
71 Lightweight Directory Access Protocol (LDAP), https://msdn.microsoft.com/en-us/library/aa366075(v=vs.85).aspx, captured at https://perma.cc/K95V-RDCQ.

Preserving Digital Objects

- Verification of each ingested object, including fixity
- Container updates (persistence module in Services web application)
- Sending a JMS message when done
- Emailing submitter when done
- Fedora ingest sequence

Replication in iRODS

- Objects and datastreams copied to redundant storage systems

For a more detailed AIP creation workflow, visit the CDR website, http://cdr.web.unc.edu/ingest-overview/.

Provide a generic or specific example of an AIP (in a diagram or schema). How does your AIP represent or account for the three main elements described in Lavoie and Gartner's diagram?

- **content information**
- **preservation description information**
- **packaging information**[72]

---

[72] Lavoie and Gartner, "Preservation Metadata," 14.

54 DIGITAL PRESERVATION ESSENTIALS

Figure 3. AIP Model

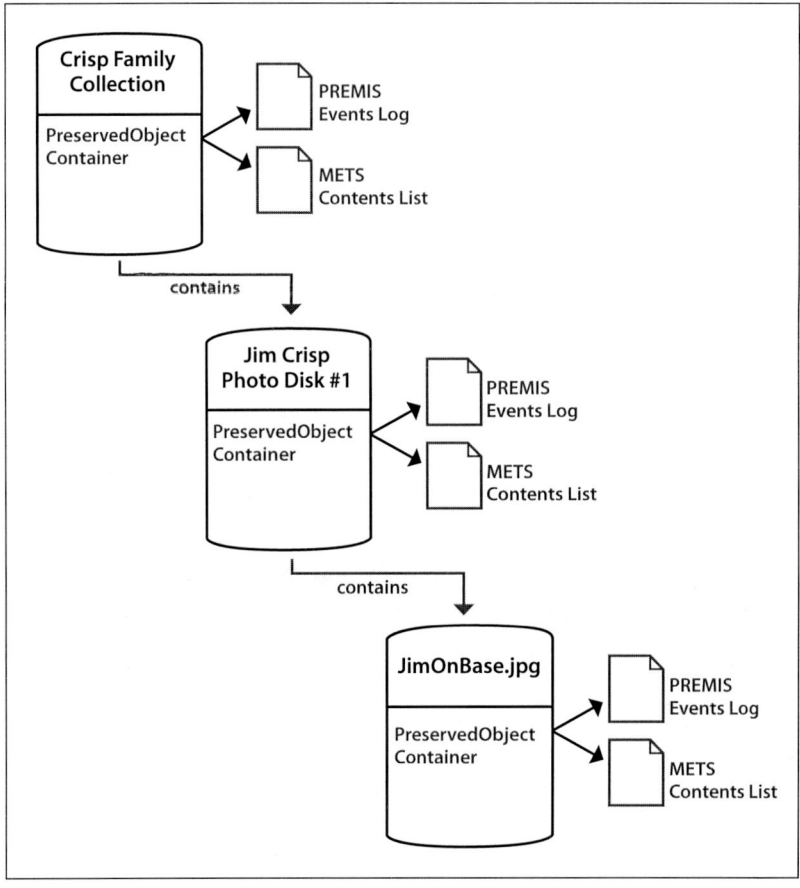

Source: https://cdr.web.unc.edu/aip-description/, captured at https://perma.cc/8KK7-MPXJ.

The model shows a sample archival information package (AIP) with a simple hierarchy. It is composed of the top-level object, the mid-level object, the smaller discrete digital object, and their associated metadata and datastreams.

The top-level object allows multiple digital objects to be grouped together intellectually; within the top-level object are smaller digital objects, often mapping to real-world constraints. It is important to note that both Crisp Family Collection and Jim Crisp Photos Disk #1 are digital objects themselves and containers of subsequent digital objects. As such, both have associated METS contents lists detailing the structure of the digital objects contained within. The lowest level of an AIP always contains individual files. All three digital objects making up the AIP make use of PREMIS events logs to record preservation events that occur to the digital objects at various levels.

While the entire structure is considered a single AIP, it can be made up of multiple submission information packages (SIPs). For example, if a user were to create a SIP called Jim Crisp Photos Disk #2 from a second disk image, it could be ingested and added to the Crisp Family Collection AIP, and then both Jim Crisp Photos Disk #1 and Jim Crisp Photos Disk #2 would be considered parts of the same AIP. That is to say, an AIP can be drawn at different levels. On one hand, individual objects can be preserved as individual AIPs; generally, though, AIPs hold an aggregated collection of objects. Aggregated AIPs are preferred because then not only are the individual objects preserved, but the relationships between objects and their underlying structure are also preserved. This is useful from at least two points of view: from a digital preservation perspective, the concepts of authenticity and trustworthiness are enhanced if an entire structure is preserved. Along the same lines, from an archival perspective, having structure and relationships preserved conveys a sense of context for the objects.

How do you perform preservation management activities on these objects? Specifically, how do you ensure the integrity of the objects in your care?

The CDR uses iRODS (integrated Rule Oriented Data System)[73] to implement its preservation storage environment. A key feature of iRODS is its ability to automate file operations. Digital objects and associated metadata files written to the CDR's storage infrastructure are automatically replicated across our storage grid and onto archival tape. One copy of every file is stored on a server administered by the Library, one copy is stored on a server administered by the campus's Information Technology Services, and the archival tape copy is stored offsite in a geographically separate location. We also automate file characterization, checksum generation, virus scans, thumbnail creation, and access copy generation. Replication and fixity checks are performed on a quarterly basis for every file in the repository, and

---

73 https://www.irods.org, homepage captured at https://perma.cc/BDU5-LELC.

results of these checks are logged in the repository. Preservation events for each object are recorded in PREMIS.

What are some of the challenges you face preserving digital objects? What are some next steps and new features you want to add to your digital preservation program?

One of the challenges we face in our efforts to preserve digital objects is prioritization, that is simply deciding which files to preserve first. Like many institutions, the amount of digital content we aim to preserve exceeds our storage and hosting capacity. Though storage has become more affordable over the past several years, hundreds of terabytes of storage is still not cheap. We believe defining preservation levels for certain digital objects, file types, and collections, and prioritizing these based on risk and long-term value, would allow us to more effectively and efficiently preserve a larger quantity of digital content over the long term.

Another challenge is hardware migration and system updates, which always loom in the not-so-distant future. Unlike a bricks and mortar building that persists for decades with regular maintenance and updating, digital preservation systems essentially have to be torn down and rebuilt every five years. In order to maintain a strong and trustworthy digital preservation system, purchasing new servers, renegotiating contracts for storage, and evaluating new software happens regularly. In a digital preservation system there is near-constant evaluation of new tools, and pieces of the infrastructure need to be upgraded on a regular schedule.

In the future, we'd like to add more normalization activities into open formats as well as virtualization as an alternative for preserving application environments.

What do you look for when evaluating tools and developing workflows for preserving digital objects? What type of requirements are essential to achieve your goals?

When evaluating tools we look for open-source tools that have grown robust user communities around them. We chose Fedora and iRODS as core components of our system not only because of the functionality they support, but because of the community around the tools. Our colleagues are our most valuable resource.

When we first started building our digital preservation program in 2008, there weren't a lot of tools available to support the workflows we identified in our environment. As a result, in 2010 we began development of the Curator's Workbench, an open-source tool that supports the preparation of digital collections. It was specifically designed with archivists in mind, incorporating features that support archival practice, from accession through arrangement, description, and SIP preparation.

Do you have any advice for repositories just starting out in digital preservation? What are some of the first steps that someone could take?

Consult with a wide range of constituents at your institution to make sure all of their needs are going to be met—including archivists, librarians, preservationists, IT staff, and potential depositors. Start small. Consider the staff and expertise you have on hand and don't plan to implement processes that you can't manage. It's possible to incrementally scale up your preservation efforts as you build capacity and expertise in your organization.

Remember that digital preservation is not just a single event, it's an ongoing process. Plan for the long-term sustainability of your program. If you plan to host your system on local hardware, be sure to budget for hardware migration every three to five years.

Don't go it alone. Try to get involved in some form of collaborative group. Some cooperative initiatives to examine include the following organizations:

- Internet Archive[74]
- HathiTrust[75]
- APTrust[76]

---

74   https://archive.org/.
75   http://www.hathitrust.org/.
76   http://aptrust.org/.

Appendix C: Preservation Metadata and Its Tools

Preservation metadata can refer to two types of information: information about preservation activities or events and information required to achieve the goals of preservation.

PREMIS (PREservation Metadata Implementation Strategies), the primary vehicle and de facto standard for preservation metadata, is capable of representing both types of preservation metadata. It can document actions that archivists, technologists, or automated scripts perform on digital objects such as ingestions, validations, and replications. PREMIS metadata can also document the actors that perform those actions such as archivists, tools, and systems. This metadata provides a record of **chain of custody** and a frame of reference critical to future rendering and access. As a **data dictionary**, it also accounts for descriptive, structural, technical and administrative information necessary to maintaining the renderability, understandability, and authenticity of digital objects over time.

PREMIS is an implementation independent data dictionary rather than a standard or schema. As a result, PREMIS, while capable of recording all necessary preservation information, is not a ready-made solution and must be configured to meet an institution's context-specific needs.

One implementation option is the PREMIS XML schema. XML (Extensible Markup Language)[77] is the lingua franca of digital preservation and digital repositories. As such, PREMIS XML is the implementation option most easily combined with other XML standards such as METS and MODS. These schemas are extensible and flexible (i.e., compatible with other metadata schemas, in the sense that they can link to or incorporate metadata in other schemas), and in some cases redundant. This allows for different implementations in practice.[78] Archivists can shape the implementation of their digital preservation metadata to fit local institutional requirements and preferences. For example, one institution may choose to use METS as a metadata wrapper, including elements of PREMIS and MODS within METS

---

77 Archivists wishing to gain more familiarity with XML should consult W3 school's XML tutorial: http://www.w3schools.com/xml/.
78 For implementation guidelines see PREMIS Editorial Committee, "Guidelines for using PREMIS with METS for exchange" (revised September 17, 2008), http://www.loc.gov/standards/premis/guidelines-premismets.pdf, captured at https://perma.cc/7DMD-B3KF.

Preserving Digital Objects   59

elements, whereas another might opt to create separate XML files for MODS and PREMIS and utilize external references, like hyperlinks, to tie the records together. In order to make these decisions, however, archivists must have a basic understanding of the purpose and uses of each schema. The following is a general overview of the schemas, outlining how they can work together to meet digital preservation needs.[79]

Figure 4. Example of preservation actions rendered as PREMIS XML events

```
    <premis:event xmlns:premis="">
     <premis:eventIdentifier>
      <premis:eventIdentifierType>URN</premis:eventIdentifierType>
      <premis:eventIdentifierValue></premis:eventIdentifierValue>
     </premis:eventIdentifier>
     <premis:eventType>
        {capture | create | message digest calculation | virus check | normalization | validation | ingest | replication | migration}
     </premis:eventType>
     <premis:eventDateTime></premis:eventDateTime>
     <premis:eventDetail></premis:eventDetail>
     <premis:eventOutcomeInformation>
       <premis:eventOutcome>
        {Pass | Fail}
       </premis:eventOutcome>
       <premis:eventOutcomeDetail>
                    <premis:eventOutcomeDetailNote></premis:eventOutcomeDetailNote>
       </premis:eventOutcomeDetail>
      </premis:eventOutcomeInformation>
    </premis:event>
```

MODS was developed as a standard to encode bibliographic information so its fields and elements should be fairly familiar to most archivists. MODS accommodates content similar to that captured in traditional archival description and EAD. MODS can also be used to describe relationships between digital objects.

---

79   For metadata schema examples and EAD crosswalks, see Appendix D.

METS is frequently used as a **wrapper** schema to connect PREMIS and MODS elements with other recorded metadata like technical and structural elements. It can be used as a container during data transmission such as ingest into a repository. As such, a METS document can incorporate all metadata components of the SIP, AIP, and/or DIP. Brian Lavoie and Richard Gartner enumerate the four types of metadata that METS can accommodate:

- A file inventory for all the files contained within the digital objects (such as still-image files, text, video or audio files);
- A section for administrative metadata, divided into four subsections, covering technical information about the files, rights management information, information on the source environment from which the object was created, and digital provenance information;
- A section for descriptive metadata, including bibliographic information and any other information about the intellectual content of the item necessary for users to find it and assess its research use;
- A structural map of the internal contents of the item, which indicates in a hierarchical manner how its various components relate to each other, thus allowing its constituent elements to be navigated by the user; this may encode its logical structure (such as the division of a book into chapters) or its physical structure (such as the ordering of pages).[80] The structural map is perhaps the most unique and crucial component from an archival perspective, because it documents the context of and relationships between objects.

As an example of combined and complete metadata profiles for digital preservation, consider a hierarchy in which MODS elements, describing digital content at an object level, and PREMIS elements, recording technical and administrative information at the object level, are embedded within METS. Combining these three metadata schemas in this way can provide a record of the objects, relationships, and processes one must understand in order to successfully preserve the object.

---

80 Lavoie and Gartner, "Preservation Metadata."

Appendix D: Metadata Schema Examples

MODS

Standard	Metadata Object Descriptive Schema (MODS) http://www.loc.gov/standards/mods/
Background	Developed in 2002 by Library of Congress
Purpose	XML schema standard for encoding descriptive library metadata
AIP component	Description information
Tools	1. Curator's Workbench 2. University of Tennessee Workbook http://dlc.lib.utk.edu/~cdeane/UTK_LIB_DLC/WB4/workbook.htm 3. Brown University MODS Editor http://library.brown.edu/its/software/metadata/

Example MODS record:

```
<titleInfo lang="english">
    <title>Pretty Picture.</title>
</titleinfo>
<name type="personal">
    <namePart>Jane Doe</namePart>
    <role>
            <roleTerm type="text">Creator</roleTerm>
    </role>
</name>
<originInfo>
    <dateCreated encoding="iso8601">2014-03-31</dateCreated>
    <place>
            <placeTerm>Denali, Alaska</placeTerm>
    </place>
</originInfo>
<abstract>
    <abstract type="findingaid">Picture, taken by Jane Doe during an expedition to Denali, Alaska.</abstract>
    <language>
            <languageTerm type="text">English</languageTerm>
    </language>
```

Selected elements mapped from EAD to MODS[81]

EAD Element	MODS Element
<did><unittitle>	<did><unittitle>
<did><origination>	<did><unittitle>
<corpname>	
<famname>	
<persname>	
<did><unittitle>	<originInfo><dateCreated>
or<scopecontent>	
<physdesc><extent>	<physicalDescription><extent>
<bioghist>	<note>

PREMIS

Standard	Preservation Metadata Implementation Strategies (PREMIS) XML schema, http://www.loc.gov/standards/premis/
Background	An RLG/OCLC working group started in 2003 and published the data dictionary in 2005. PREMIS XML schema was developed subsequently to support implementation.
Purpose	XML metadata standard to support preservation of digital objects
AIP component	Content Information: Representation Information; Preservation Description Information; Packaging Information; Descriptive Information
Tools	1. JHOVE (JSTOR/Harvard Object Validation Environment) http://hul.harvard.edu/jhove/ 2. DROID (Digital Record Object Identification) 3. New Zealand Metadata Extractor http://meta-extractor.sourceforge.net/ 4. PREMIS in METS Toolbox http://pim.fcla.edu/

---

81 Based on the EAD to Aquifer MODS map, https://wiki.dlib.indiana.edu/display/DLFAquifer/EAD+to+Aquifer+MODS, captured at https://perma.cc/Q6RM-VR5D. See also, Hypatia EAD conversion analysis, https://wiki.duraspace.org/display/HYPAT/Hypatia+EAD+conversion+analysis, captured at https://perma.cc/V9YK-ASD4.

```xml
<premis xmlns="info:lc/xmlns/premis-v2" version="2.0">
  <object xmlns:xsi="http://www.w3.org/2001/XMLSchema-instance" xsi:type="representation">
    <objectIdentifier>
      <objectIdentifierType>PID</objectIdentifierType>
      <objectIdentifierValue>uuid:ba50ff15-2468-49d5-b80f-c8dcd6e05ce2</objectIdentifierValue>
    </objectIdentifier>
  </object>
  <event>
    <eventIdentifier>
      <eventIdentifierType>URN</eventIdentifierType>
      <eventIdentifierValue>urn:uuid:8bec6ebe-21d6-465a-af4d-54ff7f5c6663</eventIdentifierValue>
    </eventIdentifier>
    <eventType>http://id.loc.gov/vocabulary/preservationEvents/validation</eventType>
    <eventDateTime>2012-03-22T00:00:00</eventDateTime>
    <eventDetail>virus scan</eventDetail>
    <linkingAgentIdentifier>
      <linkingAgentIdentifierType>Name</linkingAgentIdentifierType>
      <linkingAgentIdentifierValue>uuid:ff4fac12-0300-474b-841f-4032d041e333</linkingAgentIdentifierValue>
      <linkingAgentRole>Initiator</linkingAgentRole>
    </linkingAgentIdentifier>
    <linkingAgentIdentifier>
      <linkingAgentIdentifierType>Name</linkingAgentIdentifierType>
      <linkingAgentIdentifierValue>n/a</linkingAgentIdentifierValue>
      <linkingAgentRole>Software</linkingAgentRole>
    </linkingAgentIdentifier>
  </event>
```

```xml
<event>
    <eventIdentifier>
        <eventIdentifierType>URN</eventIdentifierType>
        <eventIdentifierValue>urn:uuid:e22a990d-d931-4229-b724-4111db116a50</eventIdentifierValue>
    </eventIdentifier>
    <eventType>http://id.loc.gov/vocabulary/preservationEvents/validation</eventType>
    <eventDateTime>2012-03-22T10:25:45</eventDateTime>
    <eventDetail>METS manifest validated against profile: http://cdr.unc.edu/METS/profiles/Simple </eventDetail>
    <linkingAgentIdentifier>
        <linkingAgentIdentifierType>Name</linkingAgentIdentifierType>
        <linkingAgentIdentifierValue>Repository</linkingAgentIdentifierValue>
        <linkingAgentRole>Initiator</linkingAgentRole>
    </linkingAgentIdentifier>
</event>
<event>
    <eventIdentifier>
        <eventIdentifierType>URN</eventIdentifierType>
        <eventIdentifierValue>urn:uuid:674401c2-454e-47bf-89ad-87bb31b31908</eventIdentifierValue>
    </eventIdentifier>
    <eventType>http://id.loc.gov/vocabulary/preservationEvents/creation</eventType>
    <eventDateTime>2012-03-13T14:45:48.741Z</eventDateTime>
    <eventDetail>SIP created</eventDetail>
    <linkingAgentIdentifier>
        <linkingAgentIdentifierType>Name</linkingAgentIdentifierType>
```

```xml
        <linkingAgentIdentifierValue>CDR Workbench</linkingAgentIdentifierValue>
        <linkingAgentRole>CREATOR</linkingAgentRole>
    </linkingAgentIdentifier>
    <linkingAgentIdentifier>
        <linkingAgentIdentifierType>Name</linkingAgentIdentifierType>
        <linkingAgentIdentifierValue>eomeara</linkingAgentIdentifierValue>
        <linkingAgentRole>CREATOR</linkingAgentRole>
    </linkingAgentIdentifier>
</event>
<event>
    <eventIdentifier>
        <eventIdentifierType>URN</eventIdentifierType>
        <eventIdentifierValue>urn:uuid:9b38f882-e300-4d72-a7d9-2f7898d35330</eventIdentifierValue>
    </eventIdentifier>
    <eventType>http://id.loc.gov/vocabulary/preservationEvents/normalization</eventType>
    <eventDateTime>2012-03-22T10:25:51</eventDateTime>
    <eventDetail>assigned persistently unique Fedora PID with UUID algorithm: uuid:ba50ff15-2468-49d5-b80f-c8dcd6e05ce2</eventDetail>
    <linkingAgentIdentifier>
        <linkingAgentIdentifierType>PID</linkingAgentIdentifierType>
        <linkingAgentIdentifierValue>admin:REPOSITORY_SOFTWARE</linkingAgentIdentifierValue>
        <linkingAgentRole>Initiator</linkingAgentRole>
    </linkingAgentIdentifier>
</event>
<event>
    <eventIdentifier>
        <eventIdentifierType>URN</eventIdentifierType>
```

```
            <eventIdentifierValue>urn:uuid:6fda
            546c-5eb5-40a4-b4ab-0ec0d40d55ce</
            eventIdentifierValue>
        </eventIdentifier>
        <eventType>http://id.loc.gov/vocabulary/
        preservationEvents/ingestion
        </eventType>
        <eventDateTime>2012-03-22T10:34:42</eventDateTime>
        <eventDetail>ingested as
        PID:uuid:ba50ff15-2468-49d5-b80f-c8dcd6e05ce2
        </eventDetail>
        <linkingAgentIdentifier>
            <linkingAgentIdentifierType>PID</
            linkingAgentIdentifierType>
            <linkingAgentIdentifierValue>uuid:ff4
            fac12-0300-474b-841f-4032d041e333</
            linkingAgentIdentifierValue>
            <linkingAgentRole>Initiator</linkingAgentRole>
        </linkingAgentIdentifier>
    </event>
</premis>
```

METS

Standard	The Metadata Encoding and Transmission Standard (METS) http://www.loc.gov/standards/mets/	
Background	METS builds upon the work of the Making of America II project (MOA2), which provided an XML document format for encoding the metadata necessary for both the management of digital objects within a repository and the exchange of such objects between repositories (or between repositories and their users).	
Purpose	XML schema standard for encoding descriptive, administrative, and structural metadata, specifically for libraries and archives[83]	
AIP component	Extensible to include PREMIS and MODS components (Content Information; Representation Information; Preservation Description Information; Packaging Information; Descriptive Information)	
Tools		1. Curator's Workbench
		2. Goobi, http://www.goobi.org/
		3. University of Illinois Urbana Champaign EchoDep Hub and Spoke Framework Tool Suite, https://www.ideals.illinois.edu/bitstream/handle/2142/14005/final_report_narrative_echodep1.pdf?sequence=2
		4. METS Navigator, http://metsnavigator.sourceforge.net/
		5. University of Florida METS Editor and Viewer, http://sobekrepository.org/software/mets

```
<?xml version="1.0" encoding="ASCII"?>
<mets:mets TYPE="WORKBENCH" PROFILE="http://cdr.unc.edu/METS/profiles/Simple" LABEL="Sample_Manifest" ID="uuid_b4780b87-2b43-4b68-9dc0-40ae3b9aff37" xmlns:xlink="http://www.w3.org/1999/xlink" xmlns:mods="http://www.loc.gov/mods/v3" xmlns:mets="http://www.loc.gov/METS/">
    <mets:metsHdr LASTMODDATE="2010-10-11T14:37:34.228Z" CREATEDATE="2010-10-11T14:37:34.228Z">
        <mets:agent TYPE="OTHER" ROLE="CREATOR">
```

---

83 http://www.loc.gov/standards/mets/.

```xml
            <mets:name>CDR Workbench</mets:name>
        </mets:agent>
        <mets:agent TYPE="INDIVIDUAL" ROLE="CREATOR">
            <mets:name>eomeara</mets:name>
        </mets:agent>
</mets:metsHdr>
<mets:dmdSec ID="uuid_5a5cc7bb-a420-4d93-8751-128728926072" STATUS="USER_EDITED" CREATED="2010-10-11T15:21:15.597Z">
    <mets:mdWrap MDTYPE="MODS">
        <mets:xmlData>
            <mods:mods ID="uuid_44e6ac83-6705-443e-8f0f-d819afee4252"/>
        </mets:xmlData>
    </mets:mdWrap>
</mets:dmdSec>
<mets:dmdSec ID="Test_file_01" STATUS="CROSSWALK_LINKED" CREATED="2010-10-11T20:26:26.870Z" GROUPID="metadata.txt">
    <mets:mdWrap MDTYPE="MODS">
        <mets:xmlData>
            <mods:mods>
                <mods:titleInfo>
                    <mods:title>Sample title</mods:title>
                    <mods:subTitle>Sample sub-title</mods:subTitle>
                </mods:titleInfo>
                <mods:name>
                    <mods:namePart>John Doe</mods:namePart>
                </mods:name>
                <mods:abstract>An essay on sample topics.</mods:abstract>
                <mods:originInfo>
                    <mods:dateCreated encoding="iso8601">2010-03-23</mods:dateCreated>
                </mods:originInfo>
```

```xml
            <mods:accessCondition type="access">¬© 2010
            John Doe. Some rights reserved under a Creative
            Commons 3.0 License for non-commercial use
            only. You may link to this URL with correct attri-
            bution, but before reproducing the presentation
            in another format, please contact the copyright
            holder. </mods:accessCondition>
          </mods:mods>
        </mets:xmlData>
      </mets:mdWrap>
    </mets:dmdSec>
    <mets:fileSec>
      <mets:fileGrp ID="OBJECTS">
        <mets:fileGrp ID="objectGrp-uuid_210d6fff-5add-422d-8f43-efc76dbca529">
          <mets:file ID="data-737120396" SIZE="22281364" MIMETYPE="application/zip" CHECKSUMTYPE="MD5" CHECKSUM="f5be640761875a7b7df189656cae1910">
            <mets:FLocat USE="STAGE" OTHERLOCTYPE="EFS_URI" LOCTYPE="OTHER" xlink:href="irods://object_vault/cdrZone/home/eomeara/staging/originals.zip"/>
          </mets:file>
        </mets:fileGrp>
      </mets:fileGrp>
    </mets:fileSec>
    <mets:structMap>
      <mets:div TYPE="Bag">
        <mets:div TYPE="Folder" LABEL="Sample Title" ID="uuid_f1241826-ee52-4404-bb0e-b4e6b1a48f0e" DMDID="Test_file_01" CONTENTIDS="file:/Volumes/share/folder/test_sample_manifest">
          <mets:div TYPE="File" LABEL="sample_title.zip" ID="uuid_210d6fff-5add-422d-efc76dbca529" CONTENTIDS="file:/Volumes/share/folder/test_sample_manifest.zip">
```

```
            <mets:fptr FILEID="objectGrp-uuid_210d6fff-
            5add-422d-8f43-efc76dbca529"/>
         </mets:div>
      </mets:div>
   </mets:div>
   </mets:structMap>
</mets:mets>
```

Appendix E: Glossary

AIP (Archival Information Package): The package to transfer and store digital objects and associated metadata. The package should contain the necessary information to access and preserve objects over the long-term. The format of the AIP may vary between systems and organizations, but it should contain the digital object and the relevant metadata.

Chain of custody: Documentation of the acquisition, transfer, ingest, and ongoing preservation of archival material. These actions could be documented by PREMIS events.

Checksum: Typically expressed as a text string or hash value, checksums are outputs generated by an algorithm and compactly express the data in a file or other data block. Checksums can be used to detect errors or changes to files stored on a computer or transferred from one computer to another since any change to the bit order of a file will result in a change to the file's checksum. Checksums are also known as file hashes or message digests.

Data dictionary: A resource that defines elements and informs use of a metadata standard.

DIP (Dissemination Information Package): The package of digital objects and metadata that is provided to the user for access.

Disk image: A bit-for-bit copy of an entire disk (i.e., forensic) or of selected files (i.e., logical) from a given storage medium (e.g., floppy disk, optical disc, hard drive).

Fixity: Refers to a file or digital object that has been unchanged or fixed. Archives want to ensure that during transfer and over time, files are not altered or corrupted. Archives will run fixity checks on documents at scheduled times, usually through a checksum.

Forensic disk image: A bit-for-bit copy of a given storage medium (e.g., floppy disk, optical disc, hard drive) which produces an exact replica of the medium's contents, including deleted files and unallocated space.

Ingest: The process of preparing material for transfer into a digital preservation environment. This could include checksum generation, unique identifier generation, and file format normalization (if necessary).

Logical disk image: A bit-for-bit copy of selected files or folders from a given storage medium (e.g., floppy disk, optical disc, hard drive).

Metadata extraction: The process by which embedded or native information about a file that is machine readable/understandable—such as file extension, file size, and file name—can be identified, understood, and repurposed from one system or software to another. A familiar archival analogy might be the transcription of creator-generated folder titles to a finding aid's folder list and to the acid-free folders in which the materials will be permanently housed.

Migration: The process of converting data from an obsolete structure to a new structure to counter software obsolescence.

Provenance: The chronology of the ownership, custody, and location of archival materials. For digital objects, this provides context for preservation actions, as well as any rights issues that might need to be considered before performing any actions on the objects.

Render: The ability to generate a digital object through the means of computer software.

Schema: A structured framework or plan. In the case of metadata schemas, it is a way to execute a specific metadata standard. For example, PREMIS XML is a schema used to execute the PREMIS metadata standard.

SIP (Submission Information Package): The package of materials that is sent to digital storage for preservation. Through archival processes, it is converted into an AIP.

Structmap: A structural map within a METS document that documents the hierarchical arrangement of digital objects, like nested folders and files.

Timestamp: Any information which indicates the time and/or date in digital materials. An archival analogy for a nineteenth-century journal might be the handwritten day, month, year, and day of the week at the top of an entry. In recording ingest information and other digital preservation events, a timestamp is ideally rendered in a standard format, such as ISO 8601, and automatically generated, as taken from an operating system.

Unique identifier: A string of characters that is associated with a digital object. A unique identifier can be unique locally, within a given system or database; or more broadly, as with universally unique identifiers or URLs. To qualify as unique, identifiers should not, with reasonable certainty, within a given environment (local or global), be unintentionally assigned to another resource. An archival analogy might be an accession number. Archives might ensure accession numbers remain locally unique by creating conventions and procedures that keep numbers from being repeated and therefore obscuring or confusing important provenance information. Universally unique identifiers (UUIDs) are strings with a mathematically very low probability of recurring. This makes them ostensibly unique across environments and allows systems and software to maintain the same distinctions (between much larger sets of data) as nonrepeated accession numbers created for archives.

Wrapper: Type of schema to wrap structural, administrative, and descriptive metadata, like METS. Some metadata wrappers also bundle content, like audiovisual wrappers. These wrappers help enable structure and connectivity between digital objects and metadata.

XML (Extensible Markup Language): Open, text-based standard for encoding and sharing information that is human- and machine-readable and widely interoperable. Archivists may be most familiar with XML in the form of Encoded Archival Description (EAD), an XML schema used to represent archival descriptive information.

MODULE 13
DIGITAL PRESERVATION STORAGE

Erin O'Meara and Kate Stratton

Module 13 Contents

Introduction • 78

Storage for Digital Preservation • 79
    Critical Issues • 79
    Best Practices, Core Principles, and Mitigation Strategies • 80

Currently Available Storage Options • 86
    Storage Solutions • 88
    Preservation-focused Storage Service Providers • 91
    Standard Storage Service Providers • 92

Storage in Practice • 93
    Documenting Requirements • 93
    Evaluating Options • 95
    Comparing Cost Models • 95
    Implementing Storage Services • 96

Conclusion and Recommendations • 98

Appendices
    Appendix A: Further Readings • 100
    Appendix B: Case Studies • 103
        University of California at San Diego Library and Chronopolis • 103
        University of Minnesota Libraries • 110
        Northern Illinois University Libraries • 116
    Appendix C: Glossary • 124

ABOUT THE AUTHORS

Erin O'Meara is head of the Office of Digital Innovation and Stewardship at the University of Arizona Libraries. Her research interests include ethnographic approaches to data management and recordkeeping, digital preservation, and archives leadership. She has previously worked at Gates Archive, the University of North Carolina at Chapel Hill, and the University of Oregon. O'Meara received her master of archival studies from the University of British Columbia in 2004. While at UBC, she conducted research for the InterPARES 2 Project pertaining to archaeological records managed in Geographic Information Systems.

Kate Stratton is the collection development archivist at Gates Archive in Seattle, Washington, where she oversees donor relations and acquisitions. Prior to joining Gates Archive in 2013, Stratton worked at the Stuart A. Rose Manuscript, Archives, and Rare Book Library at Emory University. She earned a master of science in library science from the School of Library and Information Science at the University of North Carolina at Chapel Hill in 2010.

Introduction

Imagine an archival repository that stored its physical holdings in closets, drawers, and strewn across tables. Not only would the documents and records be at risk of damage from threats like water, heat, and mice, but the archives would have trouble tracking materials and making them easily available to users.

Archives strive to establish and maintain secure and stable environments for their physical holdings, but a problem that is equivalent to the dire scenario described above can all too easily confront an archives in regard to digital objects. Archivists are increasingly responsible for the long-term stewardship and preservation of digital objects, and while digital preservation includes many activities and components, perhaps none is as central to the ultimate success of the endeavor as the storage of digital objects and data intended for preservation, since proper storage lays the foundation for other actions that archivists must take to preserve digital records.

This module provides an overview of data storage in the archival context, examining ways in which storage technologies can be selected, implemented, and used to preserve digital records. We will discuss the critical concepts, best practices, available options, and practical considerations to inform decision making and implementation planning. We will also include three case studies as examples of real world storage deployments in differing repository environments.

The primary audience for this module includes archivists, particularly those managing digital collections, as well as students learning about digital curation concepts and techniques. Though the level of experience and expertise with digital preservation and supporting infrastructures will vary greatly among members of this audience, the module is meant to be accessible to those with a general awareness of digital preservation needs and storage concepts. Throughout the module and the glossary, key terms are defined, helping all information professionals build familiarity and competence with core computer science concepts and technologies. Using the information in this module and the readings it references, repository staff can gain competence with the essential building blocks of a storage infrastructure and begin building storage services that can be trusted to preserve data and evidence about that data over the long term.

Storage for Digital Preservation

Critical Issues

The question of digital storage longevity and reliability has primarily been addressed in the computer science literature. Computer scientists have long acknowledged the fallibility of storage media, in both the short and long term.[1] As summarized by Mary Baker et al., threats to long-term storage include "obsolescence of data formats, long-term attacks on the data, and economic and structural volatility of organizations sponsoring the storage."[2] While some media have greater longevity than others, all existing storage media will eventually fail (i.e., degrade). In addition to failure of the media itself there are several other threats to short- and long-term preservation of data, including large-scale disaster, human error, component faults, media/hardware obsolescence, loss of context, attack, organizational faults, and economic faults.[3] There is no permanent or perfect storage solution to "set and forget." Storage requires **monitoring**, replacement planning, and budgeting. It also requires attention to developments and advances as new storage technologies and practices emerge.

The risks of storage failures are often acceptable in the general computing context, or acceptable with minimal mitigation (e.g., saving back-up copies of working documents to a DVD or to Dropbox). Archivists, however, have data reliability requirements that are more stringent. These requirements are most comprehensively documented in the specifications of ISO 16363 and the certification and **audit** documentation for trusted digital repositories. This standard was developed with the input of many stakeholders from the archives, library, and computer science community, and includes specific questions that

---

1 Lakshmi N. Bairavasundaram, Garth R. Goodson, Shankar Pasupathy, and Jiri Schindler, "An Analysis of Latent Sector Errors in Disk Drives," *Proceedings of the 2007 ACM SIGMETRICS International Conference on Measurement and Modeling of Computer Systems* (SIGMETRICS '07) (New York: ACM, 2007), 289–300, http://dx.doi.org/10.1145/1254882.1254917.
2 Mary Baker, Mehul Shah, David S. Rosenthal, Mema Roussopoulos, Petros Maniatis, Thomas J. Giuli, and Prashanth Bungale, "A Fresh Look at the Reliability of Long-term Digital Storage," *ACM SIGOPS Operating Systems Review*, 2006, http://arxiv.org/pdf/cs/0508130.pdf.
3 Ibid.

archivists and others can use to assess a repository's complete preservation ecosystem.[4]

The requirements for preservation storage are high because the stakes are high. Archivists are the custodians of unique or irreplaceable materials for exceedingly long time periods. They also have strong imperatives to certify and safeguard the authenticity of the materials in their care. Digital preservation policies, donor agreements, statutes, or organizational mission mandate good storage practices. Because storage failures often result in data alteration, corruption, or loss, the impact can be grave.

Fortunately, archivists, digital preservationists, and computer scientists have identified strategies, best practices, and practical processes that can inhibit the causes of storage failure and mitigate its consequences when it does occur. The remainder of this module provides an accessible introduction to the key concepts and practices that archivists can use to implement effective digital storage services.

Best Practices, Core Principles, and Mitigation Strategies

Archivists seek to implement a few simple principles and practices when determining the hardware options, configuration, and implementation for their preservation storage. While the principles are based in common sense, the manner in which an archives chooses to implement them will drastically affect the repository's likelihood of success in preserving digital materials.

Unlike paper and other physical artifacts, digital objects can, by their very nature, be easily duplicated. With the right tools and techniques, archivists can create accurate and authentic copies from the "original" file. The ability to produce near-identical copies, and the strategic management of these copies, are some of the archivist's trustiest weapons against the threats to digital storage.

Maintaining multiple copies is called **redundancy**. Redundancy allows for the possibility that even if one copy of an archival object is damaged or lost, additional copies exist to replace it. To borrow the

---

4 Steve Marks, *Module 8: Becoming a Trusted Digital Repository*. Bruce Ambacher's introduction provides a useful historical overview of the standard's development.

acronym of a Stanford-based preservation project, lots of copies keeps stuff safe (LOCKSS).[5]

Redundancy is probably most familiar in the form of **backups**. Backups are static copies of data, usually for data recovery purposes. Backups are a series of snapshots of filesystems that are used for disaster recovery. They are a key component of good operations management within a storage environment, but do not serve as an authentic copy of data in a preservation storage architecture. Many times backup techniques compress data, record deltas (what has changed on the filesystem that day), or have short retention periods on the tape or snapshot. Backups can be effective for continuity of business, but do not meet the requirements of a full **replication** strategy, as it must be implemented in a preservation storage environment.

Redundancy of copies can be enforced in storage configurations through replication, or automated copying of data from one primary storage location (e.g., server, computer) to a secondary, or several other, storage locations. Replication is distinct from redundancy in that it dynamically updates the secondary storage locations. If data is added or changed in the primary storage location, it is also added or changed in the secondary storage locations. Replication provides distinct benefits but also poses some challenges when used as part of a preservation storage system. For example, when data is intentionally added or changed, it is beneficial to have those changes automatically reflected in the secondary storage. If, however, the data is unintentionally changed (for example, through human error, file degradation, or corruption), it is far from ideal if the changes automatically overwrite more authentic or intact copies in secondary storage. For this reason, archivists must understand some core information technology concepts related to storage and, more to the point, they must collaborate carefully with IT staff responsible for implementing storage services.

A common example of redundancy in practice is **RAID**—a redundant array of independent disks. Using RAID, one can virtualize several hard drives into a logical storage box in order to achieve greater

---

5 Formally, LOCKSS is a set of technologies and collaborative agreements between partner institutions. It is used to preserve library-purchased digital content, but the acronym has entered digital preservation jargon as shorthand for the underlying principles implemented in the LOCKSS network. http://www.lockss.org/, captured at https://perma.cc/9LRY-V8YR.

redundancy. There are seven different levels of RAID, each one with its own feature sets. Most (but not all) RAID levels use parity—a way to protect data in case one of the hard drives fails in the RAID array. Understanding the concepts of RAID are helpful to communicate with system administrators and engineers as storage devices are configured for your digital collections. However, one must bear in mind that IT professionals typically see RAID as a solution to the problem of disk failure. In practical terms, IT professionals nearly always implement them in a single storage box or at least in a logical unit. For these reasons, a simple application of RAID principles will not ensure that data is geographically dispersed among two or more locations. In addition, RAID implementations typically replicate data in an automated way. When a disk fails, someone replaces it, and data is copied from the backup copy to the new drive. These factors must be borne in mind when discussing storage options with information technologists, because they can easily lead to unintended consequences.

For example, one non-ideal consequence of unchecked replication is **correlated fault**, "when one fault causes others or when multiple faults result from the same error."[6] In addition to the replication example, correlated faults can be illustrated in terms of hardware. Imagine, for example, a single laptop on which two identical copies of a document are saved. The redundancy of files provides some recourse against unintentional deletion of one of the copies. However, the hardware correlation (i.e., collocation) means that if the laptop is stolen, run over by a car, or irrecoverably crashes, all copies are lost. These issues can be mitigated by developing a carefully considered replication policy and in particular by taking backup and replication timing into careful account. For example, if incremental backup with change tracking takes place daily, but full replication and replacement take place monthly, your policy guarantees a thirty-day window to recover from any blunder. Furthermore, the implementation plan must include an audit mechanism, since any policy relying on change tracking will be complex and will require monitoring.

Archivists can counter correlated faults through **data independence**, or the intentional avoidance of correlation. Independence can

---

6   Baker et al., "A Fresh Look at the Reliability of Long-term Digital Storage."

be applied to multiple aspects of storage to achieve the safest configuration from storage media to power grids. This recommendation is the basis of the 3-2-1 rule of thumb, which recommends for preservation at least three copies of the data, stored on two different storage media (e.g., disk, tape), in at least one geographically disparate location. The National Digital Stewardship Alliance (NDSA) recommends, at their highest level of preservation, that at least three copies be maintained in three different geographic locations subject to three different disaster threats.[7] If your storage infrastructure does not follow the 3-2-1 concept, think about how you can plan, advocate, and collaborate to improve it. Could you partner with another organization to do reciprocal data sharing? Could you partner with another IT department on campus to enhance your storage footprint and features?

All components of the storage configuration and data should be monitored. Storage **monitoring** is the logging or recording of various aspects of the storage configuration and environment, including hardware, activity, and data integrity. Ideally automated, monitoring can be as simple as the tracking and comparison of file sizes and counts or as complicated as tracking all movements, changes, and recalls of a digital object. Monitoring logs should be retained over time for comparison and auditing purposes.

Closely related to monitoring is **auditing**, the process of systematically reviewing and validating outputs from the storage monitoring process. The most efficient and accurate storage auditing is automated and periodic. Storage audits can reveal important patterns related to data integrity.

Preservation services must be able to demonstrate that digital objects have not changed over time, or if they have, that changes were undertaken for specific reasons and in ways that allow software, archivists, and end users to confirm that the object is authentic. One way this is accomplished is through the recording and monitoring of **checksums**—unique identifiers used to detect errors or changes to files. For example, a preservation service might monitor a historical

---

7 Jefferson Bailey, Andrea Goethals, Trevor Owens, and Megan Phillips, The NDSA Levels of Digital Preservation: Explanation and Uses (Washington, DC: National Digital Stewardship Alliance, 2013), http://www.digitalpreservation.gov/ndsa/working_groups/documents/NDSA_Levels_Archiving_2013.pdf, captured at https://perma.cc/9R94-VPUL.

log of checksums that have been created for archival objects. If the checksum value has changed, the audit will reveal this. Changes to file **fixity** (as represented by checksums) can be an effective signal to archivists that review or repair is needed. Alerts for certain events, like fixity discrepancies, can be built into the monitoring and auditing process. Determining an audit cycle will depend on several factors: the amount of data managed, audit capabilities and processes between copies, and risk tolerance.

Monitoring and auditing activities within the storage system or actions taken on files can also be helpful for security. Monitoring logs can record the users or IP addresses that have accessed data. Auditing these logs enables archivists to verify that only approved users have accessed data or that restricted data has not been accessed by unauthorized parties. Threat analysis, a type of security audit, systematically assesses the risks and vulnerability of data and systems storing data, to maximize the security, confidentiality, and integrity of that data.[8]

Security measures like auditing can improve the longevity of the stored data, preventing purposeful attacks and unnecessary interaction with the storage environment. Preservation storage should either be inaccessible to human users (e.g., requiring software to transfer or access data) or minimally accessible to a select group of authenticated users. Common sense tells us that the fewer human hands with unfettered access to the data, the less likely inadvertent or intentional alterations or deletions of data will be. Taken further, the highest security standards suggest that no single person should have full access permissions to all copies. Encryption of data during transfer can also help prevent unauthorized users from accessing data as it is copied to storage or replicated to independent storage locations, as in the 3-2-1 scenario.

If current storage environments do not already have proper access controls, repositories should develop policies and processes that enable them. As a first step, domain network protocols such as active directory can be introduced, so that each user has a unique login, yet inherits permissions from a user group. In addition, the repository should

---

8 James Bayne, *An Overview of Threat and Risk Assessment* (SANS Institute, 2002), https://www.sans.org/reading-room/whitepapers/auditing/overview-threat-risk-assessment-76, captured at https://perma.cc/R6Z9-ZZJS.

provide users the minimum rights necessary to get their jobs done. Ideally, policies will require that system administrators and other technology staff elevate into super-user or administrator credentials when needed, so they do not accidentally alter data when undertaking routine operation. System logging within the storage environment and some sort of monitoring process should be in place to ensure there is no alteration or access of preservation masters. Ensure that logging and tracking is tied to individuals and not groups of users, including dedicated administrators. Although the full set of best practices is beyond the scope of this module, the ISO 27000 series is the international standard on information security practices and can be used as a reference point for the logic and best practices around security of digital objects in your collection.[9]

Another important component of storage longevity is continuity planning. Organizations, companies, and institutions—including archival repositories, funding agencies, and commercial storage providers—are all subject to economic pressures, reorganizations, and dissolution. It is important then that archival objects be minimally dependent on the permanence or success of any one entity. Consortia membership is one strategy to address the impermanence of funding sources or repositories. Through consortia, member institutions agree to support and contribute to a network of resources, sharing responsibilities for materials and infrastructure, persistent beyond any single organization. The potential impermanence of storage providers requires a **data exit strategy**, or the ability to retrieve archival data and metadata from the storage system. It is important that the data can be easily migrated to a new storage environment without vendor lock-in or any other hardware or software dependence.

The highest aspiration of archival storage configurations should be to meet or support the storage components specified by the requirements of a Trusted Digital Repository (TDR). The TDR guidelines are not prescriptive, and whether or not official certification is sought, repositories can aim to satisfy TDR requirements locally or use the

---

9 The ISO 27000 series currently includes seven standards and covers topics such as information system security specifications, implementation, risk management, metrics, audits/controls, and accreditation. http://www.27000.org/, captured at https://perma.cc/P9GK-FXZK.

TDR as a self-audit and improvement tool. Taking steps like these will ultimately increase long-term storage reliability, improve likelihood of preservation success, and allow end users to have increased confidence in the repository.[10]

Currently Available Storage Options

There are numerous storage offerings available on the market. Understanding the different types of storage will help you to communicate with system administrators and storage providers as you develop storage requirements and evaluate options. It is important to think about diversity of storage media in your digital preservation storage architecture as it relates to your budget, space needs, and regulatory environment. In addition to storage media diversity, think about storage vendor diversity when refreshing different parts of your storage appliances, such as drives within a storage area network (SAN). If there are problems with a specific manufacturer of drives, then this would alleviate the amount of damage or cost to replace a block of failed drives.

Some currently available options are discussed in detail below:

Optical media

Storage of digital objects on *optical discs*—reflective, laser-readable media, most familiarly compact discs (CDs) and digital video discs (DVDs)—used to be a somewhat common practice for cultural heritage organizations. Either donors transferred material to the archives via CD or that was what was available and affordable for the organization. Unfortunately, CDs and DVDs are not reliable storage media for long-term storage. Their purported shelf life varies widely based on the quality of the product itself, whether it was commercially produced or data was "burned" onto the disc from a desktop computer, as well as the conditions in which the disc is stored.[11] If you do have material stored on optical media within your collections, prioritize the transfer of the content onto stable, backed-up storage appliances.

---

10   Michael Shallcross, editor's note, in Marks, *Becoming a Trusted Digital Repository*, ix–x.
11   Fred Byers, *Care and Handling of CDs and DVDs: A Guide for Librarians and Archivists*, CLIR Publication 121 (Washington, DC: Council on Library and Information Resources, 2003), http://www.clir.org/pubs/reports/pub121, captured at https://perma.cc/F8FW-FEGE.

Hard disk or spinning disk

Hard disks, also known as spinning disks, are the most common storage medium in personal computers and network attached storage devices. **Hard disk drives** are a form of magnetic media that have magnetic platters that are read by arms that spin. Hard disk drives are vulnerable to head crash failures, which occur when the magnetic arm crashes on the platter where the data is stored. Spinning disk technology has been around since the 1950s but became more mainstream in PCs in the late 1980s as the form factor became smaller and they became less expensive to produce. Solid state is becoming more common, but spinning disk is still cheaper than solid state drives, at least in terms of the initial investment. Operating costs of spinning disk storage can be quite high since electricity is required both to power the drive and to keep the server environment cool.

Solid state

Solid state drives (SSDs) are circuit-based storage media, different from hard disks in that they do not have motors spinning disks. Because there are fewer spinning parts, solid state drives are more resistant to failure due to physical shock, but currently, they are significantly more expensive than hard disk drives (in 2015, close to 8-9 times as expensive). SSDs are more and more common in laptops, but due to the cost issue, not as common in mass storage devices implemented at the local level. SSDs are sometimes used in tiered storage solutions for flash storage, for highest availability content, and cloud storage providers typically use some element of flash storage within their storage architectures.

Tape storage

Tape storage is a magnetic storage media where data is written to plastic tape on reels or cassettes. Contemporary tape storage is cartridge based. Tape requires specialized hardware, or drives, to read the specific types of cartridges. Depending on the use, data can be written to tape and then stored offsite for offline storage, or tape cartridges can be part of a robotic tape library for **nearline storage**, or storage that is not immediately available but can be made available quickly. Many people in the cultural heritage community still use tape in some part of their storage program due to its cost effectiveness. However, tape-based storage systems can be difficult to implement, and more advanced tape storage systems will include automated retrieval and loading systems, with some lag time in making files available to an end user.

Storage Solutions

Most organizations utilize a variety of storage types based on their business needs. They will have storage allocated for rapid access to select data as well as nearline storage for files that are not accessed as frequently. Storage is configured and architected based on the business needs and data access requirements. Most organizations have tiered storage, or various types of storage for different types of use cases within their larger **data center**. Tiers are based on user requirements such as data availability, speed, and data type. The Library of Congress provided a great overview of their tiers at a recent storage conference (See Figure 1). Most archives will not be at the petabyte scale, but all archives should be familiar with the tiered model. While the Library of Congress architecture has five tiers, a small organization may wish to accommodate three of the levels in a smaller scale of processing scope and object storage. Other repositories might participate in a consortium or hosted service that implements the full tiered model (e.g., using third-party storage for an additional nearline replicant that is stored in a different geographic location).

The tiers in Figure 1 provide an example of storage architecture for different types of digital storage:
- Tier 0: high speed data housed on solid state drives for high priority and high speed transactions
- Tier 1: hard disk array that processes transactional data, like database processing or other critical computing needs
- Tier 2: hard disk array that stores active data
- Tier 3: mixture of disk and tape to store data at rest (e.g., preservation master storage)
- Tier 4: mixture of disk and tape to store backup of data

Digital Preservation Storage   89

Figure 1. Tiered Storage as implemented at the Library of Congress

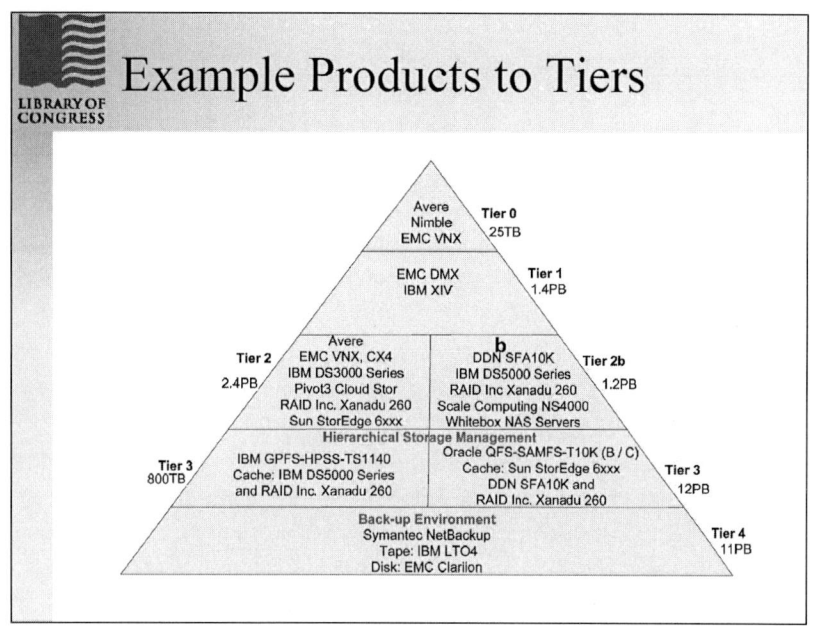

Source: Carl Watts, Designing Storage Architectures for Digital Collections Meeting, September 20, 2012, Library of Congress, Washington, DC.

Storage Management Options

Internally managed storage could be any storage architecture that is owned and managed by your own staff, whether it is on premise or offsite. The technology and the staff that manage the technology are part of the organization.

Pros
You control the entire stack. You can enforce processes and policies such as monitoring, access controls, replication strategy, fixity monitoring, and refresh cycles.

Cons
You control the entire stack. This is both a pro and a con. It is beneficial to be able to configure and manage storage exactly to your own best practices, but it is a large investment of human resources, equipment, and maintenance and replacement costs.

(cont.)

Storage Management Optoins—cont.

> **Best suited for:** large organizations that have access to staff and storage infrastructure to support management and maintenance of hardware.

Hosted storage is technology that is provided, typically under contract, on third-party architecture. Some or all processes may be administered by that third party, or some internal staff may do some system administration, like patching or virtualization.

> **Pros**
> May cost less since you do not have up-front purchase costs. If your growth rates for storage are unpredictable, this may be a lower cost as well, since you may pay only for what you need.
>
> **Cons**
> You may lose control over some aspects of management (especially data movement and access controls). Services and support may be done by a third party and may not meet your expectations or even core requirements (e.g., service levels, security, etc.). Outsiders may have access to your data without your authorization or knowledge.
>
> **Best suited for:** smaller organizations or archives that do not have technical staff to manage storage.

Hybrid storage options include those that have some storage managed internally and other parts of the architecture hosted. A good example would be hosting your own primary storage and subscribing to a digital preservation storage consortium for additional copies and geographic distribution.

> **Pros**
> This may be the best combination of preservation requirements and overall cost. This option may allow for geographic diversity, storage media diversity, or the ability to scale in a cost-conscious manner with multiple copies.
>
> **Cons**
> It is difficult to integrate processes and backup like fixity management and other synchronization processes.
>
> **Best suited for:** medium or large organizations that have staffing available for storage management, but want to have third parties manage portions of their storage needs.

Preservation-focused Storage Service Providers

We are at an exciting time in the digital preservation space: more and more service providers are catering to digital preservation needs. These services include repository software as well as storage. Consortia and distributed storage models provide potential financial and business benefits. Through these models, repositories can achieve a greater geographic diversity, better replication, and more trustworthiness when working at a scale larger than a single repository.

While the following list is not normative, it describes some library and archives-specific hosted services available at the time this module was written.[12]

Chronopolis is a digital preservation data grid hosted at UCSD Libraries with **nodes** at the National Center for Atmospheric Research (NCAR) in Colorado and the University of Maryland's Institute for Advanced Computer Studies (UMIACS). It is essentially a preservation-oriented private cloud using replication management and fixity management across nodes. Chronopolis's use case is for a preservation copy that is not intended for active retrieval and use. You would still need to have an active copy of your data hosted elsewhere. The easiest way to ingest content is through DuraCloud, but you can subscribe directly to the service. Fixity management in Chronopolis is done through the use of ACE Audit Manager software at each node. Checksums for each digital object are compared across the nodes regularly.

DuraCloud is a service provider that offers several preservation storage solutions. They provide backup services that could be a part of your digital preservation storage architecture, as well as preservation storage that is stored across several storage providers. DuraCloud is a service provided by the DuraSpace organization, which promotes long-term access to digital content. The DuraCloud offering is configurable. There are several storage options, including Amazon S3, Amazon Glacier, and Chronopolis. Fixity management is done through Amazon S3. DuraCloud also

---

12 Chronopolis, https://libraries.ucsd.edu/chronopolis/about/index.html; DuraCloud, http://www.duracloud.org/; DPN, http://dpn.org/; Preservica, http://preservica.com/; Arkivum, http://arkivum.com/; libdata, http://www.digitalpreservationsoftware.com/digital-preservation-solutions/libdata-digital-preservation-storage/.

hosts digital preservation software, Archivematica, that can be integrated with a DuraCloud storage solution.

Digital Preservation Network (DPN), is a federated preservation storage solution with five geographically distributed replication nodes, each a preservation repository. DPN provides data integrity checking and file repair for dark storage of your assets. DPN also offers succession planning to ensure the persistence of objects independent of any single member institution. DPN officially launched in March 2016.

Preservica is a digital preservation software that incorporates some storage configuration and management functions. Depending on the edition, storage options can include Amazon S3, Amazon Glacier, on premise, or hybrid.

Arkivum is a storage provider that provides hosted storage in its own data center (currently only in the United Kingdom) or managed storage in your own facility. Their infrastructure is tape-based. Arkivum's unique features that relate to digital preservation are their data escrow service and the insurance policy offered against data loss. Arkivum has a 100% data integrity guarantee. They also have indemnity insurance on the data they store and will provide payment if there is any data loss. Arkivum can also place a copy of your data store in escrow with a third party as an additional protection measure.

libdata is a new storage offering from libnova, a Spanish company entering the digital preservation market. Their storage appliance is geared toward robustness and high storage density.

Standard Storage Service Providers

In addition to preservation-oriented storage providers, non-preservation-oriented cloud and other distributed storage options could be part of your larger infrastructure. Amazon, Google, Microsoft Azure, Rackspace, and many local storage providers host data centers and provide storage at a relatively affordable cost. In some instances, using their services can provide financial advantages, especially if you do not have the staff to administer multiple data centers. For archives who continue to grow, this option can help enable rapid growth without major infrastructure planning and cost, like data center peripherals and additional hardware. Local policies or regulatory requirements that govern your organization's data storage must be carefully considered when planning for the use of hosted storage technologies.

Storage in Practice

This section discusses practical approaches for storage planning and procurement, with the specific goal of helping archivists and repositories determine what type of storage and storage service providers best meet local needs.

Documenting Requirements

As a first step, document the minimal requirements that you expect your storage configuration to meet. These requirements should reflect the concepts, best practices, and principles discussed above, such as replication, redundancy, independence, and the avoidance of correlated faults. Consider which of your requirements are "must haves," necessary to fulfill the mission of your organization; "should have," in the long-term best interest of your mission; or "nice to have," optional or surpassing your stated mission.

Archivists will often be part of a larger IT project to procure storage for a parent organization or partner. Documenting and prioritizing requirements specific to the archives will enable you to communicate effectively, as a stakeholder in a larger group, and the archival perspective can enrich discussions and concerns that affect all parties. Discuss and compare requirements with other stakeholders to understand how they work with the larger group's needs and requirements. If procuring storage on your own, work with colleagues in IT to learn about their requirements and procurement processes. They will almost certainly have experience and perspectives that will translate and inform the archival domain.

Here are some key questions to consider when defining specific requirements for a storage system:

Levels of replication: How many copies do you need to keep? For preservation (e.g., replicants)? For access (e.g., derivatives)?

Frequency: How often will mirroring take place? When will incremental backups vs. full replication be used? How long will copies be kept before deletion, and how will your repository guard against the possibility of correlated faults?

Storage space: How much storage space do you need to accommodate your current holdings? How much do you expect your holdings to grow over the next twelve, twenty-four, and thirty-six months? Consider your response to the levels of replication requirement when calculating current and projected space requirements.

Access needs: How will different manifestations (preservation, access) be used and accessed? What actions will different users (researchers, archivists, technology staff) need to take on each manifestation to complete their work successfully?

Formats: What types of file formats do you manage? What formats do you want to preserve? Will you provide the same level of preservation for all formats?

Auditing requirements: What is your risk tolerance? At what level will you audit/monitor fixity (e.g., file, directory)? How frequently will you require audits? Will you audit comprehensively or through sampling? Consider the data processing required to achieve your projected audit cycle.

Existing infrastructure and software: What are your current technology systems and software? How do you expect or need your storage to interact with existing systems? Are there integration points or blockers with existing systems?

Tiered storage: Do all of your manifestations and digital objects need the same level of access, replication, and monitoring? Can digitized copies or access manifestations be managed with less rigor? Will a tiered architecture provide any cost savings in your context?

Contractual or statutory obligations: Does your donor agreement contractually commit to specific levels of preservation or privacy? Are there any legal statutes governing the rights or privacy of the subjects of your collections? Are there any statutes affecting the geographical location of your storage (i.e., jurisdiction) or response to data loss?

Evaluating Options

The requirements developed above can be used as a matrix to evaluate and compare available storage options. Review the standard **Service Level Agreement** for each option against your requirements. Can any be immediately removed as options? Would a combination of proposed solutions be better?

Weigh the ability to meet requirements against other business considerations, such as the resources needed to support the storage over time. What staff, hardware, and software are needed in addition to existing available resources? Would managing storage on premise compared to a hosted solution add to or alleviate these resource needs? Are there consortial storage options available? If so, how might consortial storage fit into your architecture?

Comparing Cost Models

Planning and projecting storage costs for a growing digital preservation program can be challenging. There are multiple variables, including growth rates, storage prices, and changes to technology and requirements, which are difficult to predict. The composition of holdings, including file formats, are also hard to predict (especially born-digital materials from donors, since archivists do not always have the opportunity to suggest or require specific file formats).

There are several in-depth cost planning projects to look at as you are planning for storage costs and making a business case. Some repositories choose to use a cost recovery service with specific customers to help fund their infrastructure. Other repositories lower costs by sharing with other internal customers, like a research computing cluster on a campus or another department with similar storage needs. Several resources provide planning guidance regarding costs associated with digital preservation. The California Digital Library's Total Cost of Preservation Model and the resources identified in the 4C Project cost models are particularly helpful.[13] There are several considerations that factor into the preparation of cost projections.

---

13 California Digital Library, Total Cost of Preservation (TCP): Cost and Price Modeling for Sustainable Services, 2015, https://wiki.ucop.edu/display/Curation/Cost+Modeling, captured at https://perma.cc/L436-HKDX. 4C Project: Collaboration to Clarify the Costs of Curation, Summary of Cost Models, http://4cproject.eu/summary-of-cost-models, homepage captured at https://perma.cc/5WD8-YWJJ.

Initial purchase: Initial cost can vary greatly, depending on hardware and software costs, and availability of existing hardware that can be repurposed. Existing infrastructure may consist of racks to hold storage, switches, cabling, HVAC in the data center, etc. Installation costs can also vary widely. Consider whether you will do it yourself or have a third party or the storage vendor install for you.

Maintenance and support: Costs can also vary widely for maintenance, depending on the solution you choose and how you handle the service. You will need to determine whether you will handle all maintenance and service costs with your own staff resources or subscribe to a maintenance and service contract through the storage provider. Most people will have some form of a service contract with the vendor. Cost for support can rise dramatically, especially if there are "end-of-life" cycles or time-limited warranties defined by the storage vendor or hardware manufacturer. For hosted storage, how much is the maintenance, or is it bundled in your monthly or annual fee?

Refresh and replacement cycle: Standard refresh and replacement cycles should coincide with maintenance agreements. Once networked storage outlives its maintenance contract, it can be risky and expensive to maintain. Plan for refresh or replacement every three to five years.

Other factors: Other factors affecting cost projections include, but are not limited to, data storage growth, staff salaries, and consortial membership commitments. These will be unique to each institution.

Implementing Storage Services

Once you have documented your requirements, evaluated options, and investigated costs, your repository is ready to make some decisions and implement storage services. Implementation of storage should be conducted in phases. Hardware and peripherals will need to be procured, or hosted storage contracts will need to be reviewed and signed. Once the storage is online, it will need to be configured. Configuration could mean different things, depending on your architecture. Local storage configuration could include extensive configuration like switches, routers, operating system, domain, logging, and replication. Hosted storage could include access, API configuration to applications, and monitoring configuration. Data upload or migration would be addressed in a separate phase once configuration is complete. Ensure you have the right tools, people, and processes in place before data is transferred to the new environment.

Once a storage solution is selected, costed, and approved, there are additional considerations specific to local implementations. For example:

Location of data center: Will the data center be housed on premises or externally? Data centers are space- and resource-intensive, with specific environmental (temperature, humidity) and power requirements.

Networking: How will your preservation storage be networked, or connected and accessible, to other hardware and users? What security protocols will protect the preservation storage from networked devices and users?

Staffing: Do you have the staff to manage the storage you need? If so, do they have the skills to manage the storage hardware and operating system of the solution you have selected?

Interoperability: How does the storage architecture integrate with your core applications like digital preservation software, digital collection software, and collection management applications? Are there specific configuration or implementation paths required to enable interoperation?

There are additional weightier and more individualized issues that, depending on local context, may be worth considering in your storage selection, procurement, and implementation.

Regulatory: What are your organization's regulations regarding data security, data stewardship, and privacy, like HIPPA, data privacy laws, contractual agreements with donors, or other regulatory laws related to data storage? Are any of the potential storage solutions out of alignment with those policies? Conduct research to understand if parts of your collection have restrictions concerning where they can be stored (state, country).

Ethical: What are some of the nonbinding, but important ethical or professional best practices that you need to consider for your digital stacks? What are the terms of service with cloud vendors who may access or move your data without any needed approval? If you are looking at a hosted data center, do you need a locked cage and dedicated engineer to access your data at the remote site? Do you have any sensitive data—human rights collections, activist collections, whistleblower collections, or classified data inadvertently kept by public officials—that may be prone to penetration/attack? If your repository holds such materials, access controls must be carefully defined, implemented, and monitored.

Contractual: What are the terms of service, as documented in your Service Level Agreement, with your data provider? With your donors? Is your data being stored with other customers' data and would it be made available to an attorney if their data was part of a legal discovery process? Are there built-in parameters in your contract to prevent this?

Security: What is the presumption of security by your donors? What does your donor agreement say about data stewardship? What have curators verbally promised to donors? What is the risk if the data is accessed by unauthorized users?

Financial: How does your cost model change if you need to have segmented/physically separate stores for sensitive and public archival data? What is your current funding model for storage?

Conclusion and Recommendations

The composition of archival collections is increasingly digital. In response to this shift, archivists need to prepare just as thoughtfully for the long-term storage of their digital objects as they have their paper and artefactual objects for years. A well-considered storage strategy is critical to the success of overall preservation and accessibility of digital objects. Understanding the concepts and stakes involved in storage planning will enable repositories to make informed decisions and construct a best-fit solution suited to their unique requirements and constraints.

Digital Preservation Storage 99

The following actions will play a critical role in any well-considered storage strategy:

- Identifying the ways in which potential threats such as disaster, human error, hardware faults, media obsolescence, and loss of context pose specific storage risks
- Understanding core principles and practices from both the archival/digital preservation community, and from the information technology community, that support the development of trusted storage services
- Communicating with IT staff and others who also have an interest in and knowledge of storage issues, and articulating digital preservation needs and requirements in a collegial fashion
- Researching the particular storage options available within a repository or consortium (these may include local storage, preservation-focused storage providers, or standard/cloud-based storage services)
- Developing and documenting storage needs and requirements as a set of criteria that can be used to evaluate and help select storage options
- Projecting and planning storage costs based on past experience and future growth expectations
- Implementing storage services in a phased fashion, carefully considering problems and issues identified when storage needs and requirements were defined
- Evaluating, monitoring, and auditing the storage environment and services

Every archives owes its constituents a healthy and enduring environment in which to store digital materials, to enable ongoing access to what they transferred to us. As the case studies in Appendix B illustrate, archivists are rising up to meet the storage challenge in a variety of ways. Using the information in this module and the further readings as a starting point, every archives and archivist responsible for digital collections can work toward these goals for their digital preservation environment.

Appendix A: Further Readings

4C Project: Collaboration to Clarify the Costs of Curation. Summary of Cost Models. http://4cproject.eu/summary-of-cost-models. Captured at https://perma.cc/5WD8-YWJJ.

AVPreserve Storage Vendor Profiles. https://www.avpreserve.com/papers-and-presentations/cloud-storage-vendor-profiles/. Captured at https://perma.cc/L55R-QDBZ.

Beagrie, Neil, Andrew Charlesworth, and Paul Miller. *How Cloud Storage Can Address the Needs of Public Archives in the UK*, 2015. http://www.nationalarchives.gov.uk/documents/CloudStorage-Guidance_March-2015.pdf. Captured at https://perma.cc/8AXC-ZETD.

Bairavasundaram, Lakshmi N., Garth R. Goodson, Shankar Pasupathy, and Jiri Schindler. "An Analysis of Latent Sector Errors in Disk Drives." In *Proceedings of the 2007 ACM SIGMETRICS International Conference on Measurement and Modeling of Computer Systems* (SIGMETRICS '07). New York: ACM, 2007, 289–300. http://dx.doi.org/10.1145/1254882.1254917.

Baker, Mary, Mehul Shah, David S. Rosenthal, Mema Roussopoulos, Petros Maniatis, Thomas J. Giuli, Prashanth Bungale. "A Fresh Look at the Reliability of Long-term Digital Storage." In *ACM SIGOPS Operating Systems Review*, 2006. http://arxiv.org/pdf/cs/0508130.pdf.

Bayne, James. *An Overview of Threat and Risk Assessment*. SANS Institute, 2002. https://www.sans.org/reading-room/whitepapers/auditing/overview-threat-risk-assessment-76. Captured at https://perma.cc/R6Z9-ZZJS.

Brown, Adrian. Digital Preservation Guidance Note 2: Selecting Storage Media for Long-Term Preservation. National Archives, 2008. https://www.nationalarchives.gov.uk/documents/selecting-storage-media.pdf. Captured at https://perma.cc/95FA-6SCF.

Byers, Fred. *Care and Handling of CDs and DVDs: A Guide for Librarians and Archivists*. CLIR Publication 121. Washington, DC: Council on Library and Information Resources, 2003. http://www.clir.org/pubs/reports/pub121. Captured at https://perma.cc/F8FW-FEGE.

California Digital Library. Total Cost of Preservation (TCP): Cost and Price Modeling for Sustainable Services. 2015. https://wiki.ucop.edu/display/Curation/Cost+Modeling. Captured at https://perma.cc/L436-HKDX.

Consultative Committee for Space Data Systems. *Audit and Certification of Trustworthy Digital Repositories.* Washington, DC, 2011. http://public.ccsds.org/publications/archive/652x0m1.pdf. Captured at https://perma.cc/8J63-TBEA. Chapters four and five cover digital object management and infrastructure and security risk management.

Factor, Michael, Ealan Henis, Dalit Naor, Simona Rabinovici-Cohen, Petra Reshef, Shahar Ronen, Giovanni Michetti, Maria Guercio. "Authenticity and Provenance in Long Term Digital Preservation: Modeling and Implementation in Preservation Aware Storage." https://www.usenix.org/legacy/event/tapp09/tech/full_papers/factor/factor_html/. Captured at https://perma.cc/2YD8-4VRP.

Hedstrom, Margaret. "Digital Preservation: A Time Bomb for Digital Libraries." *Computers and the Humanities* 31, no. 3 (May 1997): 189–202. http://www.uky.edu/~kiernan/DL/hedstrom.html. Captured at https://perma.cc/KX96-97PT.

InterPARES Project. "Records in the Cloud." http://www.recordsinthecloud.org/. Captured at https://perma.ccQH27-P6L5.

Library of Congress Digital Preservation Meetings
- http://www.digitalpreservation.gov/meetings/storage12.html. Captured at https://perma.cc/K583-HUH6.
- http://www.digitalpreservation.gov/meetings/storage13.html. Captured at https://perma.cc/CQP5-ERK8.
- http://www.digitalpreservation.gov/meetings/storage14.html. Captured at https://perma.cc/LP7Y-MHU5.
- http://www.digitalpreservation.gov/meetings/storage15.html. Captured at https://perma.cc/YMY5-9ZZM.

MetaArchive Cooperative. *Getting to the Bottom Line: 20 Cost Questions for Digital Preservation.* http://www.metaarchive.org/public/publishing/ma_20costquestions_final.pdf. Captured at https://perma.cc/9U95-UYL2.

Minnesota Historical Society. *Report on Digital Preservation and Cloud Services*, April 2013. http://www.mnhs.org/preserve

/records/docs_pdfs/Instrumental_MHSReportFinal_Public
_v2.pdf. Captured at https://perma.cc/AJE2-RXDP.

Minnesota Historical Society. *Electronic Records Management Guidelines*. March 2012. http://www.mnhs.org/preserve
/records/electronicrecords/docs_pdfs/LongTermPreservation
-v5march2012.pdf. Captured at https://perma.cc/HP6N-69SM.

Minor, D., D. Sutton, A. Kozbial, M. Burek, M. Smorul. "Chronopolis Digital Preservation Network." *International Journal of Digital Curation* (June 2010). https://libraries.ucsd.edu/chronopolis
/_files/publications/chronopolis_dcc_revised.pdf. Captured at https://perma.cc/NLK5-7VQK.

Phillips, Megan, Jefferson Bailey, Andrea Goethals, Trevor Owens. *The NDSA Levels of Digital Preservation: An Explanation and Uses*. 2013. http://www.digitalpreservation.gov/ndsa/working
_groups/documents/NDSA_Levels_Archiving_2013.pdf. Captured at https://perma.cc/9R94-VPUL.

Rosenthal, David S., Daniel L. Vargas, Tom A. Lipkis, Claire T. Griffin. "Enhancing the LOCKSS Digital Preservation Technology." *D-Lib Magazine* 21, no. 9/10 (September/October 2015). http://www.dlib.org/dlib/september15/rosenthal
/09rosenthal.html. Captured at https://perma.cc/7P2S-Q6ZA.

Rosenthal, D.S., D.C. Rosenthal, E.L. Miller, I.F. Adams, M.W. Storer, E. Zadok. "The Economics of Long-term Digital Storage." *Memory of the World in the Digital Age Conference*. Vancouver, BC, 2012. http://www.lockss.org/locksswp/wp-content/uploads
/2012/09/unesco2012.pdf. Captured at https://perma.cc
/XBY8-HT9M.

Rothenberg, Jeff. *Avoiding Technological Quicksand: Finding a Viable Technical Foundation to Digital Preservation*. CLIR Publication 77. Washington, DC: Council on Library and Information Resources, 1999. http://www.clir.org/pubs/reports/
reports/rothenberg/pub77.pdf. Captured at https://perma.cc
/5QKM-AQXL.

Appendix B: Case Studies

This appendix provides edited interviews illustrating three different approaches to digital preservation storage: a large research library using a hosted storage service, a research library using a locally developed storage service, and a medium sized university using a cloud storage service. The case studies provide a short biography of each interviewee, along with answers to questions posed by the authors of the case study to the interviewees.

University of California at San Diego Library and Chronopolis
Interviewee Roles
Tim Marconi is the IT operations manager at the University of California at San Diego (UCSD) Library. He supervises a team of seven staff who support many IT systems in the library, ranging from everyday systems like email, interlibrary loan, and lending systems; as well as more complex and unique resources such as a DAMS (digital asset management system) and a research data curation program. These systems require a great deal of storage and general computing support.

Sibyl Schaefer is the digital preservation analyst/Chronopolis program manager at UCSD. She ensures that Chronopolis operations function as expected across three country-wide nodes: one at UCSD; one at the University of Maryland Institute for Advanced Computing Studies in College Park, Maryland; and one at the National Center for Atmospheric Research in Boulder, Colorado. The position requires communications management, reviewing documentation needed for things like TRAC/TDR auditing, and tackling questions such as versioning. Chronopolis has a partnership with DPN, the Digital Preservation Network, which is where a lot of their development focus is right now.

Tell us about your repository and the types of digital objects it stores. More specifically, can you describe how UCSD Libraries stores its digital assets for long-term preservation?

We have two different systems that we work with. One is the DAMS, that is the UCSD, Hydra repository. It will be Hydra Fedora at some point, but that migration has not happened. The DAMS is preserved in Chronopolis, so they are two different systems. Chronopolis can also preserve objects that are not necessarily in the DAMS. So, we talk about both of those and they are different entities.

The DAMS repository is Hydra[14] and eventually Fedora.[15] Our backend is homegrown, using our own repository. We will be going to Fedora eventually, hopefully by the end of 2016. It consists of just under 100,000 objects. It includes research data sets, images, documents, video and audio recordings. All are in the same system and a search can go through everything, but you can also go specifically to assets: digitized versions of collections covering topics such as art, film, music, history, and anthropology through the libraries; or our research data collections, which is through our data curation program if you specifically want to scope for research data.

What is the general extent of your digital holdings and what type of growth patterns are you seeing annually?

The size of our holdings on disk is about 25.5 terabytes. We increased by approximately 5 TB over the last year, due to the addition of research data.

When we transitioned from our completely homegrown systems to Hydra, we put a freeze on ingestion for about a year in 2013-2014. We were pretty static in our preservation assets and our file system was not growing that much. When we launched the new DAMS based on Hydra, we saw an increase—a lot more data more quickly. We opened the floodgates and said "ingest away." I expect it to continue to grow, because the data sets we are getting are much larger. We are not getting that many more collections, but the data that we are getting, especially with regards to research data, are big. We are getting big data, and preserving it is a challenge.

With growth patterns, we have been growing just under 5 TB every year. I expect that to increase, maybe 5–7 or 7–10 TB annually, depending on how large the datasets become.

We are also currently in a holding pattern for our special collections and born-digital records and archives. They will be large. We will need to make some good decisions as to what we want to put in the DAMS and preserve. We have whole hard drives. Do we want to make

---

14 See https://projecthydra.org/, project homepage captured at https://perma.cc/P9ZH-D3F7.
15 See http://fedorarepository.org/ , project homepage captured at https://perma.cc/PH9D-Z2V7.

all of that available? I don't think so. I think it has to be curated down a bit. The originals will be in the DAMS. We expect that anything born-digital, TIFF files, for example, will be there and will be large.

What type of storage do you use to preserve your digital objects?

Primary storage for preservation objects is an EMC Isilon. The full cluster raw is 2.1 PB, which comes out to about 1.6 PB useable. It runs OneFS, which is the Isilon operating system. It is **networked attached storage** (NAS) that is mounted and run here locally on campus. The Isilon is on premise.

Previously the relationship was one where Chronopolis was a service provider. That has changed because the Chronopolis management has come under the library purview, so now it is an in-house operation. Storage used to be managed by the San Diego Supercomputer Center (SDSC), but now it is managed by the library. The Chronopolis Program Manager also used to be an SDSC position, but is now under the library. It has definitely become more of an in-house service that we run for our own needs, but also to offer to outside institutions.

How did you make the decision to use this storage type?

In 2010, we had "white box" storage, storage that we purchased from a reseller. It was a bunch of servers with a lot of disks, a lot of 2 TB drives. It was a very economical way to get a lot of storage back then. We had 13 or 14 file servers that all had 2 TB drives and they were running RAID 10. We had lots of storage but we were having drive failures in those machines. We had a lot of reliability problems and we were scared about data loss. We did not end up losing any data, but we were worried that we were going to lose some. We also started to run into the upper limits of the actual file systems. The biggest file system we could get on them was 37 TB and our staging group was approaching that all the time. We would keep giving them more space and ultimately they were going to expand outside of the 37 TB we could give them. At that point we needed to find a solution. We did not want to add another server, another map point, with the data in two completely different places for them to manage. Part of the decision was wanting to satisfy our customers, making it easier for them to manage the data that they were putting in and working on. Part of it came from a preservation standpoint. We were really worried about how these hard drives were failing and if we were going to lose data.

Around 2012, we got a refurbished Isilon, because they are very expensive. It was night and day in terms of management. Now we had one cluster to manage. We had very few drive failures, and when they did, it did not matter because we could lose 36 drives and still be okay because of the way load balancing and node balancing works with regards to data parity. So, we were comfortable knowing that three copies of the data were spread across the five different nodes and we could survive a lot of different failure types. Another benefit is that we got to be on one filesystem—it was a 320 TB filesystem at the time—so we just had to worry about that 37 TB cap that we were running into. Ultimately, we transferred everything to our Isilon and it worked really well for us for three years. Then we were running near the hardware end of life. In 2014, we did a large search again to see if there were any hardware and software solutions out there, and there are many that would meet our needs, but we came back to not having to touch the data again. The Isilon offers a pretty seamless transfer; if you buy another cluster you just join the cluster to your existing one and all of the data moves over without us having to touch anything. We did not have to do any rsyncs; all the data just moved over. That definitely made us want to stick with that. We were able to get a five-year support contract with this one, so we will not have to do this exercise again until 2020, fingers crossed.

Overall we evaluated ten storage vendors to see the different products that could work. There are definitely cheaper ways to do this, but the ease of management—the fact that I do not have to dedicate a storage administrator to this—is worth it. It happens to work well as the storage for Chronopolis, as well. It is harder when we are pricing Chronopolis since it is the most expensive storage that Chronopolis uses. Our other two sites kind of act as subcontractors to us, so they have a set budget that they need to work within to get storage. That is not really dictated by us, but is more what they can purchase with that cost and what they can run in-house without it being cumbersome. Those are the two main qualities we are looking for in storage. But it is all spinning disk, we are not using any tape.

Do you see cloud storage as a part of your storage architecture, and in what role (understanding Chronopolis is distributed storage as opposed to cloud)?

From a system administrator point of view, one of the things that comes up pretty often is that people will say: Chronopolis is our backup. That is frustrating because Chronopolis is not our backup; it is our preservation dataset. Backup, in a system administrator context, is to make sure we have a backup of our data. We would like to get our datasets into a cloud provider, but we have not yet done that because our datasets are large, and we would start with something that is just under 30 TB. Most cloud storage providers want a hard drive instead of transferring via the network. We would like to take advantage of this snow ball from Amazon and put a backup of our operational data in Amazon and do nightly backups, so we could recover from the cloud using that. It would be relatively inexpensive. It is not saving us money, but we need backup somehow and that would provide us with it. Using cloud for backup purposes works well for us. From a preservation aspect, with regards to fixity checking and everything else, that is what we have Chronopolis for.

We have a lot more storage here than we do at the other two nodes of Chronopolis. We need to determine a strategy for what gets distributed across Chronopolis and what does not. The reason is each node does not have 2.5 petabytes—it is around 300 TB at the other nodes. There are cost implications to increase the storage. If we do fill up our Isilon, then we do need to look at a solution to back up our data, and cloud services could be a fantastic way to go for that. But I do want to stress that we would not consider that a preservation service.

What is your opinion on storage media variety and number of copies of your data?

I love the old adage of the 3-2-1: three copies of the data on two different formats and at least one in another location. But, we do everything with spinning disk, we do not have a tape infrastructure. The amount of data we are talking about right now—the investment we would have to make in tape—we could easily get cloud storage for a fraction of the cost. We have no interest in going to tape, but if there was another format, like if DOTS did exist,[16] that would be nice. Technologies like that sound great, if they end up becoming a reality, but most of these new technologies have never been released for production use. There are a lot of predictions with blu-ray and increased density, but without blu-ray robots and the rest of the needed infrastructure, it's hard to know what would serve us well. I would like to put our data on another format at some point, but I do not have another format that I believe in right now.

I strongly feel that three copies is the minimum; I would like to have more. I do count protection mechanisms, when you are considering RAID that is inherent in storage. I do count those as copies. If you say, "my non-RAIDed copy of this is the same as a triplicate erasure coded system like Isilon or NetApp," I do not think those are apples-to-apples comparisons since there is some protection inherent in these filesystems that should be considered. One copy from one Isilon is not data protection, though. You need to have multiple copies.

For Chronopolis infrastructure, everything we do is on spinning disks, but the systems are all different. So we are not using the same hardware. Even though we do not have variations in type of hardware, there is variation in the actual manufacturer. With regards to the number of copies, we have three distributed copies; but it is likely there are actually more copies since we are using the Isilon here and there is redundancy at the other nodes, too. We do not count those copies. But when we have to do some type of restorative action, that redundant copy is the recommended file to use for the restore before pulling from another node. So there is an assumption there is another copy of the file at each node.

How are you managing fixity across digital objects?

In Chronopolis, we run ACE Audit Control Environment. There is an instance of it running at each of the three nodes. It registers each item at the file level when they are ingested into the Chronopolis system. It also tokenizes them, which is a level on top of that, which protects the object in case anyone changes the checksum. The files are audited every 45 days. As the size of Chronopolis grows, we will be keeping an

---

16 DOTS (Digital Optical Technology System) is a digital storage media for long-term preservation developed by Kodak. It is in the development stage and not yet available to consumers. http://group47.com/what-is-dots/, captured at https://perma.cc/G64W-WHSR.

eye to make sure that is a reasonable time frame. The 45-day cycle is a pretty aggressive schedule.

How are you thinking about long-term budgeting and costs for your storage needs?

We take the number that we paid for the Isilon in 2015 and divide it by five since that is the supported number of years. The library budgets that amount to their server replacement budget for the next five years, so that at the end of those five years, the library will have the total amount of money that it paid for the Isilon this year to spend in 2020 for storage replacement. The question is: are we sure we will pay the same amount we paid this time and will we need the same amount? No, because there will be growth in collection size and changes in technology, like density differences; but the library will have a set sum of money to then work with. If the library needs to supplement and request more funds, then it will, but right now that is the model for replacement. The library projects for five years; it does not want to project too far out because the landscape changes so rapidly. We want to be able to adapt if we need to.

What are the biggest challenges you are facing with regard to digital preservation storage?

It takes a while to get content from the DAMS into Chronopolis and it has not been done on a frequent basis. Hopefully, we can figure out how to version what we have versus doing wholesale data replacements into Chronopolis.

There is a lot of talk in the digital preservation world that has a tone of a lack of hope: "we're never going to be able to do this," and "it's so hard." It is hard to overcome that and to not get overwhelmed by what could happen in five years: what if every dataset is 40 TB, and what are we going to do if that becomes the new normal? No one really knows, but if we get caught up in the *what if*, we will not be thinking about what we need to be doing right now. It is good to plan ahead as much as you can, but I think lately there has been a lot of defeatism there. Some of the challenge is to maintain hope that it is going to happen. There is a lot of born-digital stuff that we want to preserve and we can do it. Technology is evolving and things are going to get better.

Some of the other biggest challenges are things you already know: there are going to be budgeting challenges with how much things will cost. You will get a lot of people telling you that the cloud is free and why are we not just using it. We are also challenged to explain why digital preservation storage is different—explaining what fixity is and why we need it. Other people may ask: well, Amazon says they hold three copies of everything, so why is that not our preservation strategy? Education can be difficult, too.

Another challenge is file format instability and the dependencies we have around research data that we preserve that has been generated on proprietary software or software that is very specific to a field or even a lab (developed by the lab itself). We have not delved into what it means to preserve data that was generated by that software and/or can only be accessed by that type of software. The DAMS was originally for digitized materials and those file formats are so standardized and popular like TIFFs. But some of the research data file formats I am more concerned about, especially the raw data. Of course that brings up the question of whether we want the raw data versus data that has been processed.

University of Minnesota Libraries

Interviewee Role

Carol Kussman is a digital preservation analyst at the University of Minnesota Libraries. Kussman's position is within the Digital Preservation and Repository Technologies department, which is part of the Data and Technology division of the Library. Her role can be interpreted as the intermediary between people within the libraries who want to have digital objects preserved and the digital preservation environment that we have. She tries to figure out the needs of both sides and how her department can address them. This is a fairly new position within the libraries; she has been in the role for two years.

Tell us about your repository and the types of digital objects it stores.

The University of Minnesota includes many repositories that accept the digital content for which we are responsible. Our institutional repository is currently using DSpace, another repository is Drupal based, and another uses ContentDM. We also have digital objects that are not stored in specific repositories. With the variety of backend systems in use it makes it challenging to understand the full range of materials that we need to preserve. This is compounded by the fact that most of those systems accept almost any type of digital object. DSpace, in particular, allows you to put anything into it. Our DSpace repository includes a wide variety of materials including word documents, PDFs, power points, audio/video files in various formats, GIS files, data files, CAD information, and images in various formats including TIFFs, JPEGs, and Jpeg2000.

Other repositories have a more controlled environment. The materials in our ContentDM repository are mostly digitized material, mostly image files. Pretty much everything that comes into ContentDM has been pre-approved to be digitized and preserved. To assist in our endeavors with other repositories, a list of suggested file formats and associated levels of preservation are shared with depositors. An example of this is the policies for the University Digital Conservancy (UDC), our institutional repository.

The levels of preservation help define how much work we will do on the back end to preserve files. At this point, some file formats are easier to preserve than others. As a whole, we are working on trying to figure out in more detail within our department what file formats we are most comfortable with. We are working with the UDC in trying to build out our policies so we have a wider framework that will work to address the formats we may find ourselves needing to preserve. We need to be able to work with what these repositories take in and understand how we are going to preserve them on the back end.

What is the general extent of your digital holdings and what type of growth patterns are you seeing annually?

We currently have about 300 TB of files/data/information and we expect it to grow at about 100 TB or more per year. Materials come from deposits into the various repositories by individuals, departments, units, or others on campus, but they also come from grant projects that the libraries are involved in.

Most of the repositories allow anyone associated with the university to self-deposit materials. The majority of reports, presentations, and documentation are created digitally and the repositories provide ways for sharing these materials. In the past, reports, presentations, and documentation of university activities were sent to the archives in paper form but these types of materials are created digitally and can be self-deposited by anyone associated with the university at any time throughout their time here. Because of this, materials are constantly being added.

Grant projects are also a major source of digital files. The libraries have many grant projects that involve creating digital materials, whether that is digitizing analog materials or working on born-digital video projects. Successful grant projects lead to exponential growth of the amount of digital content under our care.

What type of storage do you use to preserve your digital objects?

We are using a combination of spinning disk and tape. The spinning disks are on a Sun/Oracle storage frame and we are using LTO-6 tapes.[17]

Is this storage hosted or on premise?

The spinning disks are onsite and we make the tape copies ourselves. The tape copies are full copies rather than just the changes which are stored offsite. To create full copies we follow a two-week cycle of creating tapes and sending them offsite. Currently we are in charge of the storage equipment, and how and when multiple copies are made; however, this responsibility may change over time.

How did you make the decision to use this storage type?

At this point in time, the server and tape combination was the best solution for us. We looked for high-quality hardware and software. Also, because we were purchasing hardware, we wanted to make sure that what we were purchasing was going to be by a vendor or service that had a good reputation. This is why we chose the Sun/Oracle combination. LTO tapes were also a known product with quality and a good reputation. As with all storage equipment, newer versions of tapes replace older versions of tapes; with LTO tapes, the cycle and support for these different versions is known. We know when new versions of tapes will be released and how long the older versions of the tapes will be supported and by which machines. Having that knowledge and

---

17 Linear Tape-Open (LTO) is a widely implemented and nonproprietary magnetic tape format. The tape is contained in a cartridge, and at the time of writing seven versions of the LTO format had been released.

understanding of what is being supported, for how long, and when, is good to know because if the vendor you are using is going to stop producing things, you may find yourself out of luck if you cannot use your tapes or equipment any longer.

Do you see cloud storage as a part of your storage architecture if you aren't already using it? If you are using it, what role does it play?

We are not using cloud storage now, and part of it has to do with the amount of content we do have. Similar to the issue of creating full backups and how long it takes with the amount of data we have, sending that amount of data to and from the cloud is cost-prohibitive, especially if you do need to access it more than you would when using it as a dark archive that is accessed only in emergency situations. The price-capacity ratio has not hit a sweet spot yet in terms of price and value for us, so it does not fit our needs now. There may be some things in our care that can go into the cloud or the cloud could be used for certain purposes; but for right now, with the way we are structured, it is kind of an all or nothing thing. With the amount of content we have, it just has not worked for us yet.

What is your opinion on storage media variety and number of copies of your data?

Having content on more than one type of media is good; you do not want to have all of your eggs in one basket. As discussed before we use two different types of media: spinning disk and tape. We have a minimum of three full copies at any one time. Actually, with the way that tape backups are created, there is always a copy onsite, a copy in transition, and a copy in storage, increasing the number of copies we have. Fortunately, we have not had to refresh things or rebuild our infrastructure yet. We have had to pull things off, remove them based on storage getting full, and have had to do some backups after moving things to a different server. Having reliable copies of your data is essential to all of these types of activities.

How are you managing fixity across digital objects?

We monitor or check fixity across our digital objects at the file level using MD5 checksums.

We monitor fixity any time files are being moved—writing the files to tape, for example. If we move files from one server to another we also check the fixity of the files before and after the move. So, anytime we do a move, we check to make sure the move was successful. We also try to do an annual check of everything on the disks that has not been moving, which is a continual process. If necessary we can check the fixity of certain collections or repositories at any time to make sure we check the files on the disks at least once a year.

We are running MD5 checksums per file. We have had discussions with people who wonder why we are not using some version of a SHA-x algorithm. In our situation, we are not worried about people going in and compromising the files and trying to spoof an MD5. We feel that MD5 is secure enough for our purposes and it fulfills the purpose of understanding if something has changed over time or after a file transfer and has the least amount of processing overhead.

How are you thinking about long-term budgeting and costs for your storage needs?

We are well aware of the increase of digital materials at the libraries, which will only continue to grow. To assist with the long-term management and support of these materials, we are looking into how we can share this responsibility with others. For example, the Digital Preservation and Repository Technology department currently does not have the responsibility of preserving published materials in digital form. Some of these and other library materials are currently within HathiTrust.

We are also working with Digital Preservation Network (DPN) to better understand their goals and model and to build partnering relationships around digital preservation efforts. In general we are looking at what is going on with these types of larger networks and looking to see if there are ways to share preservation services and effort. However, with the wide variety of materials in our care we need to understand rights and sharing requirements. Not all of our materials can go offsite. We need to balance these needs if we share responsibility with another organization.

We are also constantly monitoring hardware and software needs and must continue to make solid decisions when purchasing future equipment.

What are the biggest challenges you are facing with regard to digital preservation storage?

The biggest challenge related to digital preservation storage is that the information is not going to stop coming; we are going to keep receiving materials in digital form, and most likely faster than ever. How do we deal with that amount of information?

Think about video files. The amount of storage space required for storing HD video is huge! There are lots of grant project where digital video is being created; do we know what will be kept? The working copies as well as the final edited versions? What are we responsible for preserving?

Just this past year our institutional repository started accepting research data. Currently, we have a smaller research data collection, but that could grow to be larger. How do we address concerns around those collections? There are going to be formats that are going to be more proprietary and unique than what we have seen before, and they could be large datasets.

We are challenged to get people to understand that there are consequences to creating digital files that require long-term preservation. These consequences include a constant need for monitoring, which requires time and resources. It is still very common to hear things like "storage is cheap" and "we can just get more." But think about it: our file sizes are getting larger, which means the space required to save a single file has increased. A digital image taken today on our phone takes up a lot more space than an image taken five years ago on a digital camera. Storage costs themselves may be coming down, but file sizes are going up; eventually you may need more storage for a smaller number of files. Trying to change this opinion—that storage is always cheap—is a challenge because you cannot always just go buy more. Cost, as always, will be an issue depending on what we need to do going forward.

Another challenge is simply the fact that the libraries will be asked to preserve more and more information. To address this, we are working on policies that document what we are able to preserve and what we are required to preserve. These policies will help the libraries communicate to all of our partners what we will and won't be able to do.

In general, it is challenging to put all the moving pieces together. There are a lot of moving pieces and a lot of people that need to work together and systems that need to work together. Making them all talk to each other can be challenging.

Northern Illinois University Libraries
Interviewee Roles

Lynne M. Thomas is the head of special collections at the Northern Illinois University Libraries and was the co-primary investigator on the Digital POWRR Project during the initial project submission phase for the IMLS grant. Her role in the repository is largely providing content. She collects contemporary literary manuscripts that are often electronic and reside in an Islandora repository.

Jaime Schumacher is the director of scholarly communications at Northern Illinois University Libraries and manages Huskie Commons, the institutional repository. Jaime was the first project director for the initial Digital POWRR Project grant through IMLS, and is now co-primary investigator on the project, now funded by the NEH.

Tell us about your repository and the types of digital objects it stores.

The institutional repository, Huskie Commons, is a DSpace instance, and the place where we collect a lot of the institutional output of NIU, such as peer-reviewed scholarly materials, student scholarly output, departmental publications, theses and dissertations (digitized and born-digital), as well as some datasets. The library's other repository, geared toward special collections in digital form, is a Fedora-Islandora-Drupal instance. It contains items like our dime novels that have been digitized on our Nickels and Dimes digital collections site. It also serves as a dark archive for materials that are still in copyright and need to be preserved but cannot yet be made public, such as the literary manuscripts of science fiction and fantasy literature. The bulk of the digital projects were created over the past ten years through various digitization grants and multi-institution grants. This includes materials from the Abraham Lincoln–Lincoln/Net, a site about the golden age in Illinois. It also includes materials from websites related to Southeast Asia, some regional history center holdings, and University Archives material. There are about five of us in the library that are content contributors to the Islandora repository. Currently, we do not have a staff member managing the technical side of the Islandora repository, since the digital collections curator recently left the library.

All assets within both repositories are stored in DuraCloud, but we may be moving storage to Amazon Glacier due to cost and shrinking budgets. We decided to use DuraCloud because Fedora and DSpace can synchronize with it, so the process of preserving the objects would be seamless. They currently have been force dumping digital objects into DuraCloud (manually loading files into DuraCloud) and are working toward an automatic synchronization.

What is the general extent of your digital holdings and what type of growth patterns are you seeing annually?

In Huskie Commons we currently have just over 2,600 digital objects occupying 9 GB of space. It is a fairly new repository so what we are seeing right now is a lot of batch uploading of items like our dissertations and theses. We have seen pretty quick growth, but we anticipate that leveling out a bit. In the future we will see a lot more one-off deposits, where faculty members and students deposit their scholarly output into Huskie Commons. Part of that is driven by the fact that NIU recently passed an open access policy that requires all faculty members to deposit their peer-reviewed scholarly work into the institutional repository, thereby making it open access. Increasing awareness of and compliance with that policy will drive a portion of the repository's growth in the future. We are not anticipating the doubling and tripling that we have been seeing over the past couple years as we got off the ground.

The last time we surveyed the Fedora/Islandora repository was when we were trying to pull together our digital preservation case study for the Digital POWRR grant. We figured that we had between seven and ten TB of materials that needed to be preserved. That includes fifteen years of legacy digital projects all together. We didn't expect a ton of growth, but my colleague and I are in the process of applying for a CLIR Hidden Collections grant which would allow us to quadruple the number of dime novels we have digitized at a higher resolution. If we get that grant, then our storage needs are going to at least double very quickly. This will be paid for in part out of the grant in the first few years, but eventually we will have to pay the maintenance fees on that.

We also have another donor-driven project of digitizing sheet music that will be undertaken at some point, which will also massively add to this. We are at the stage now where we are just skirting toward having enough infrastructure to do slow mass digitization of public domain materials in our collections; if we had been at a bigger place with bigger visibility, this would have been done already. So, it is going to grow by a lot.

We have both born-digital and digitized materials. The Regional History Center and University Archives, in particular, have a ton of born-digital university records. My science fiction subset is also a growing area. We are working with the major professional organization for science fiction writers (the Science Fiction and Fantasy Writers of America) and we expect to be taking in their digital files at some point, but they have been holding back in order to organize before submitting them. We have and will continue to get materials that are born-digital as well. They are all held in the same repository and managed together. We don't have separate spaces for born-digital and digitized materials.

The materials in Huskie Commons, the institutional repository, are primarily now born-digital with the exception of the theses and dissertations that are being digitized and ingested. The past three years of theses and dissertations are born-digital.

What type of storage do you use to preserve your digital objects?

For storing and back-up we have a NAS here locally that is backed up elsewhere on campus, and beyond that it is whatever we can get up into DuraCloud. From there we feel like it is in really good hands because they have robust preservation checks and balances going on at DuraCloud. Right now we have the DuraCloud plan that is in both Amazon Glacier and S3, going forward it will just be Glacier. In Rare Books, for the Science Fiction stuff in particular, we have an ongoing practice of using external hard drives, too. We have access copies that we keep here onsite that are locked-down external hard drives for those files, and we update them periodically. They are not technically backups, they are access copies, but they are a safety measure. We have had some issues with backups in the past. In recent memory, we have had some issues with the NAS and the campus-level backups. We are trying to manage those issues while still maintaining file integrity.

How did you make the decision to use this storage type?

For the NAS, it was what was available and pretty much the only option at the time. As a result of the POWRR project we were able to test out and be trained on DuraCloud. We had a very favorable view of it. We found it pretty easy to use and very robust. Once we got our administration's attention by saying, "these backups here locally are not enough; we need to get this original, unique material off of campus and out somewhere else where it can be better taken care of," then we got the funding, and it was pretty much a natural decision to go with DuraCloud, driven by the fact that both Fedora and DSpace could be synced with DuraCloud.

One of the aspects of the initial Digital POWRR grant was to examine and hands-on test both front-end management solutions and back-end storage. The decision making basically came down to: What works with what we already have and is relatively cost effective? That was how we ended up with DuraCloud.

What is your opinion on storage media variety and number of copies of your data?

My opinion is that the more that you can afford, the better, but we cannot always afford as many as we would like. The preservation standard, I think, is about six copies. We are just not in a position to be able to manage six copies. I would be happy with two. I would be ecstatic at three, personally.

I think two is sufficient, if one is in a geographically different location—definitely one offsite. We are in tornado country. Having one of your storage locations be not on campus would be good. If the campus gets hit by a tornado, you want one of the copies of your data to be elsewhere.

Our repositories are smaller, compared to some. It is nice to have a local preservation copy so that if there is a failure, you are able to restore it yourself, rather than jumping through the red tape to get your stuff back from wherever it is—in our case, DuraCloud. It just would be faster and less painful. For us, though, it is a no-brainer to have your stuff offsite in someone else's hands, as long as that someone else is trustworthy.

How are you managing fixity across digital objects?

The short answer is really only sorta-kinda. We are functioning at the good-enough level of digital preservation. We are never going to meet the gold standard, because we are not budgeted or staffed in a way that that would be possible. What we do generally is look for solutions that deal with checksums and automate getting and checking checksums on our digital files, which DuraCloud does. That is the main tool that we use.

Beyond that, I'm not sure if we have implemented using Data Accessioner yet. We are working toward doing it routinely, but I'm not certain that we have gotten that far yet. We are still in the place where what happens before the point of ingest is still a little fuzzy. We are still building procedures for the preparatory stuff, to get things ingested into the Islandora/Fedora repository.

We are running checksums through DuraCloud and we are trusting that if the time comes where we need to restore our local copies of the repository, that those checksums will all match up. We have faith in the system.

The nice thing is that usually you can choose what sort of algorithm is going to be used in creating checksums for managing the fixity. If you can get the right people talking to each other and agree on an algorithm, that will help with making it a bit easier, down the road, so that you're not trying to figure out, "Ok, here's a checksum, but what the heck created it?"

We have gone with MD5. Basically, anytime we move from one system to another we just have to make sure that it is compatible and will work with MD5 checksums. One of the minor advantages to being under-resourced is that you can make choices and therefore not be stuck with analysis paralysis. You can say, "Well, this is what we're doing and that cuts out a whole bunch of other options, because this is what we're doing."

If we needed to move from one system to another, we would recreate the checksums in the new instance and do a full comparison. We have not had to do it yet. Knock on wood.

How are you thinking about long-term budgeting and costs for your storage needs?

In the past, building up to the 7–10 TB of material that is now managed in the one repository, those items were being collected and created without too much thought to the costs of the long-term preservation. One of our current management practices is to think through cost implications when a project is proposed, trying to put real numbers to it, instead of saying "Sure, we can handle a few more gigabytes or a few more terabytes." Both the content providers and the systems folks here at NIU are trying to get a handle on what sort of storage needs we are looking at and what those might cost. Looking at numbers and being honest about that is a big step in the right direction. We are really being squeezed in terms of budget.

When we think about long-time budgeting and costs, not only is it important to have hard numbers—we need to be obnoxious about advocating for digital preservation and paying for those hard numbers, to keep pushing and pushing and pushing. I [Lynne] don't ever shut up about this when talking to my boss, who is currently the interim dean of libraries. When we hire our new dean, I will be obnoxious. We will be asking about that as an interview question and we talk with people across campus about this too, because these are campus-wide projects.

The institutional repository takes in materials from across campus, so this is something that needs to be centrally funded through campus. It can't be just the library's money problem. It has to be the entire campus's money problem. A lot of this is just being willing to be that squeaky wheel. I [Lynne] am a tenured faculty member so I have the ability to be slightly more forward than my colleagues who are not yet tenured or not on the tenure track. I leverage that as hard as I possibly can, because it is important. I am one of those people that will just talk about this as something that is important and explain why; I try to convince people that it is in their own interest to protect the cultural heritage value of library materials. I frame it that way, rather than in terms of risk management. I talk much more about the data losses that will come if we do not solve the problem rather than say, "the library needs money."

We live in boom and bust cycles. What tends to happen is that in the boom years we upgrade our tools or we advance our software—that's when we make the big changes from system to system—because there is a little more room for outlay. We have to build our systems with the assumption that we are going to have a good run of bust years. Any time we talk about storage costs, having those hard numbers is hugely important because we have to know what our baseline is so that we don't go below it.

What are the biggest challenges you are facing with regard to digital preservation storage?

Filling the technically inclined positions that are currently empty. Those are the folks that do the hands-on moving about of stuff. We turn files over to the people in those positions and then I don't have to think specifically about the preservation function since our processes were designed to support it. That is how we are structured. But, if I am turning my files over and they don't go anywhere, that is a problem. I think making sure that we get to the point where we have a process that is relatively seamless to get our materials ingested and then duplicated out into our storage—that is our challenge. We just have not achieved that yet, and that is really the biggest stumbling block right now. We need to automate that and make it easy somehow.

We focus a great deal of attention on helping people who don't understand this, helping them understand why this is important enough that we have to provide resources to make it happen, talking to them in a way that makes it real for them. Many people face this challenge, regardless of what resource level they have.

Advocacy is always hard. It is always more difficult when you are dealing with folks who are not specialized in the thing that you are specialized in. Then you have a double gap. You have to cross the "advocacy is often uncomfortable" gap and you have to cross the "we are not always speaking the same language even if we use similar terms" gap. When we talk to systems folks, for instance, we talk about multiple copies and digital preservation in a general sense and they say, "Well, we have backups. Isn't that enough?" And we have to cross the information gap to say, "No, backups are not enough. That's barely a baseline for what we are talking about." And we have to cross the gap of "this is also an uncomfortable conversation, because advocacy is often uncomfortable."

When you look at Special Collections and talk to people who are not in this field and say, "I have these medieval manuscripts that I need to preserve and that's going to cost money," they can understand that. If you then say, "I have these contemporary manuscripts that are in digital form that I need money to preserve," they might respond, "Computers are ubiquitous. They're everywhere, so just make copies." They don't really understand the preservation portion of that. And that makes it harder for donors to write checks for it.

It is a lot easier to convince someone who is willing to write your library a check to buy you something pretty, like a medieval manuscript or a fancy book. It is always easier to convince people to drop a chunk of change on a tangible thing that they can see, something they can have their names on, especially if it is the kind of tangible thing that other people would be envious of. It's a lot more difficult to say, "This digital preservation hub is sponsored by [name of donor]." It is a much harder sell. But in the long run that is the sort of thing that we need to consider because we can't afford not to think about any and all ways to raise money for this sort of thing and find sustainable funding. This is not one and done. Most libraries are modeled on one and done. This is how the whole serials crisis happened in the first place. You buy a book once, it's a purchase that sits on the shelf forever. The cost is sunk and you don't have to repeat it. With serials and with digital preservation, there are ongoing costs and they keep going up. We have to find ways to structure our budget to take that into account.

Appendix C: Glossary

Audit: Process of systematic review and validation of storage environment, for example, the analysis of monitoring logs.

Backup: Static copy of data, usually for data recovery purposes.

Checksum: Typically expressed as a text string or hash value, checksums are outputs generated by an algorithm and compactly express the data in a file or other data block. Checksums can be used to detect errors or changes to files stored on a computer or transferred from one computer to another since any change to the bit order of a file will result in a change to the file's checksum. Checksums are also known as file hashes or message digests.

Correlated fault: A fault caused by another fault or multiple faults resulting from the same error.

Data exit strategy: A known ability or plan for retrieving archival data and metadata from a storage service or system. Examples include ability to export data and metadata in structured, interoperable, nonproprietary formats like XML.

Data independence: Noncorrelation or unshared characteristics of storage between files. For example, the use of multiple storage media (e.g., disk and tape) or multiple geographic locations.

Data center: A large group of networked computer servers typically used by organizations for the remote storage, processing, or distribution of large amounts of data.

Fixity: "Unchangedness" of data, usually evidenced by identical and persistent checksums generated from the same file over time.

Hard disk drives: A form of magnetic media that have magnetic platters that are read by arms that spin.

Monitoring: Logging or recording of various aspects of the storage configuration, including hardware, activity, and data integrity.

Digital Preservation Storage

Nearline storage: Storage that is not immediately available but can be made available quickly.

Network Attached Storage (NAS): Storage server containing one or more storage drives often arranged into storage containers or made redundant through RAID.

Node: A machine that is connected to a backup server and one or more devices used in backup, archive, and hardware security module (HSM) operations. Devices attached to storage nodes are called remote devices because they are not physically attached to the controlling backup server.

RAID: A redundant array of independent disks.

Redundancy: Creation and retention of multiple near-identical copies of the same data.

Replication: Automated copying of data from one primary storage location (e.g., server, computer) to another or several other storage locations. Replication is distinct from redundancy in that it dynamically updates the secondary storage locations.

Service Level Agreement: A contract between a service provider (either internal or external) and the end user that defines the level of service expected from the service provider.

Tape storage: A magnetic storage media where data is written to plastic tape on reels or cassettes.